jQuery Mobile

DEVELOP AND DESIGN

Kris Hadlock

D1456079

jQuery Mobile: Develop and Design
Kris Hadlock

Peachpit Press

1249 Eighth Street
Berkeley, CA 94710
510/524-2178
510/524-2221 (fax)

Find us on the Web at: www.peachpit.com
To report errors, please send a note to: errata@peachpit.com
Peachpit Press is a division of Pearson Education.
Copyright © 2012 by Kris Hadlock

Acquisitions Editor: Michael Nolan
Project Editor: Rebecca Gulick
Development Editor: Robyn G. Thomas
Contributing Writer: Jay Blanchard
Technical Reviewer: Jay Blanchard
Production Coordinator: Myrna Vladic
Compositor: David Van Ness
Copyeditor: Gretchen Dykstra
Proofreader: Patricia Pane
Indexer: Valerie Haynes-Perry
Cover Design: Aren Howell Straiger
Interior Design: Mimi Heft

ISBN-13:   978-0-321-82041-9
ISBN-10:   0-321-82041-X

9 8 7 6 5 4 3 2 1

Printed and bound in the United States of America

To my wife, Lisa, who carried our first child while I wrote this book.
Only true love can withstand the amount of time that it
takes to write a book while having a new baby.
And to my son, Lucas, words cannot
express the love I feel for you.

ACKNOWLEDGMENTS

There are many people I would like to thank for the opportunity and help they gave before, during, and after this book was being written: Neil Salkind, for helping me navigate the world of publishing and for his support while I was writing. Robyn Thomas for her patience. Jay Blanchard for stepping in when needed and providing excellent technical reviews. Rebecca Gulick for helping to move things along. Michael Nolan for working out the details. All my customers, for understanding how busy I've been. And, of course, Peachpit for giving me the opportunity to write for you.

ABOUT THE AUTHOR

Kris Hadlock has been a web developer and designer since 1996, working on projects for companies such as SPIN Magazine, IKEA, United Airlines, JP Morgan Chase, Canon, and Phoenix Children's Hospital, to name a few. Kris is a featured columnist and writer for numerous websites and design magazines, including Peachpit.com, InformIT.com, IBM developerWorks (*www.ibm.com/developerworks*), and *Practical Web Design* magazine. His other books include *Ajax for Web Application Developers* and *The ActionScript 3.0 Migration Guide*. He is the founder and lead developer-designer of Studio Sedition (www.studiosedition.com), specializing in the fusion of form and function.

CONTENTS

INTRODUCING THE **FUTURE** OF **WEB DEVELOPMENT**

Smartphone, tablet, and e-reader statistics are showing an unprecedented adoption rate, making the mobile web a very hot topic and requiring a new set of skills from web developers and designers. Mobile device usage is skyrocketing; according to Nielsen's third-quarter 2011 Mobile Media Report, "44 percent of U.S. mobile subscribers now own a smartphone device, compared to 18 percent just two years ago." That's more than double in two years, and "the number of smartphone subscribers using the mobile Internet has grown 45 percent since 2010." As for tablets, in June 2011 AMI-Partners (Access Markets International) forecasted that "tablet adoption among businesses with between 1 and 1,000 employees will grow by 1,000 percent by 2015."

Let's not forget e-readers, which are becoming very affordable and are more advanced then ever, increasing in shipment volume, as "year-over-year growth was 167%" according to International Data Corporation (IDC). With the introduction of the latest Kindle, mobile Internet access is now becoming a normal experience.

With these increases in adoption rate, there will no doubt be high demand for web developers who can create rich mobile web experiences. The jQuery Mobile framework gives web developers a quick and easy way to create mobile web experiences, making the mobile web space hard to ignore.

WHY jQUERY MOBILE?

As a web developer, you don't have to use the jQuery Mobile framework to create a mobile web experience. So why use it? For starters, the framework is built on the highly respected and widely used jQuery core and jQuery user interface (UI) foundation. It's currently sponsored by companies such as Mozilla, Palm, Adobe, Nokia, BlackBerry, and more. Plus, it works seamlessly across all popular mobile device platforms. The jQuery Mobile team is actively and regularly offering new releases, blogging about new features, and keeping their comprehensive online documentation up to date.

Most web developers and designers agree that browser and cross-platform testing is something they would rather not spend their time on. Imagine all of the devices that could potentially be accessing your mobile website. Then imagine having to test all of those platforms each and every time you build a mobile website—this would be painstaking and incredibly time-consuming. jQuery Mobile gives you this support from the start, as the team prides the framework on its approach to supporting a wide variety of mobile platforms. The framework is built on clean, semantic HTML, which ensures compatibility with a majority of web-enabled devices.

The framework also includes accessibility features, such as WAI-ARIA (Web Accessibility Initiative-Accessible Rich Internet Applications), a technical specification published by the World Wide Web Consortium regarding the increase of accessibility of webpages, which are integrated into the framework to support screen readers, such as VoiceOver on Apple iOS and other assistive technologies. Simply including the jQuery Mobile framework in your website unobtrusively transforms your code from semantic HTML into a rich, interactive, and accessible mobile experience using jQuery and CSS. As you'll see throughout this book, the jQuery Mobile approach makes mobile web development incredibly easy, quick, and efficient, leaving the platform and browser testing up to the jQuery Mobile team.

jQuery Mobile isn't exclusively for web developers; web designers have access to the jQuery UI, which provides complete design control over mobile web applications. Built-in UI widgets, such as list views, dialogs, toolbars, search mechanisms, and a full set of form elements, are all customizable via the theme framework. Later in the book, you'll also learn about ThemeRoller, which lets you create up to 26 theme swatches using a simple, web-based interface. User experience (UX) designers also get some love, with access to stencils for OmniGraffle and Visio. And, of course, if you want to get geeky with it, the application programming interface (API) is available to web developers. As a web developer, you can configure defaults, handle many different events, and work with several exposed methods and properties.

An emerging community is helping to support the framework with a number of third-party apps and frameworks that you can use to build jQuery Mobile apps. In addition, jQuery Mobile compatible plug-ins and extensions are popping up to help web developers integrate custom widgets and add capabilities to the existing core functionality.

One very important third-party framework is blurring the line between native and mobile web-based development. As an HTML5 app platform, PhoneGap allows you to author native applications using web technologies. With PhoneGap, your web applications can easily be ported into native apps that can do things like retrieve contact information, access cameras, use geolocation, store data, and much more. To learn more about PhoneGap, visit phonegap.com. There's even a section in the jQuery Mobile online documentation about it. With these sorts of possibilities, you no longer need to program multiple versions of a native application. This makes native application development less desirable, because the same application you develop for an iPhone would need to be completely redeveloped for Android, Black-Berry, Windows Mobile, and others. Oh, and don't forget that every new release will need to be updated for every one of these different platforms. The jQuery Mobile framework provides mobile web experiences that rival native application development by giving you instant access to web applications and websites via the web browser, eliminating the need to download and install mobile applications.

WHO THIS BOOK IS FOR

This book is for people who have basic HTML experience and are interested in creating mobile websites using the jQuery Mobile framework.

WHO THIS BOOK IS NOT FOR

This book is not for people who have never created a webpage.

HOW YOU WILL LEARN

In this book, you'll learn by doing. Each chapter includes sample code and descriptions to give you a deep understanding of how things work. You can also find the code samples on the book's website (www.peachpit.com/jquerymobile).

WHAT YOU WILL LEARN

This book will teach you everything from the basics of how to create pages to custom-theming them and developing your own jQuery Mobile content-management system with WordPress and Drupal. By the time you finish this book, you'll be a jQuery Mobile expert.

WRAPPING **UP**

The jQuery Mobile framework is a powerful framework that is supported by mobile industry leaders. It can easily be added to an existing website to create a mobile web experience that is not only touch-friendly, but also supported on a majority of the leading mobile platforms as well as handicap accessible. Design control, page transitions, widget integration, scripting, API access, and much more are all at your fingertips through this framework's easy-to-use features and built-in progressive enhancement techniques.

SUPPORTED
jQUERY MOBILE
PLATFORMS

The jQuery Mobile framework supports the majority of modern desktop, smartphone, tablet, and e-reader platforms. Rather than spending your time testing multiple devices, you can rest assured that you're offering support for many platforms from the start. This is because the jQuery Mobile platform takes a progressive enhancement approach, which not only brings rich interactive experiences to devices, but also provides support for older browsers and phones. When a browser fails to recognize certain HTML5-specific code, the webpage renders as a simple, yet functional webpage. Users on older phones or browsers are familiar with a limited web experience, therefore this approach still renders an acceptable basic HTML webpage in these cases.

Currently, Android and Apple iOS are the leading mobile operating systems. Android has the largest operating system market share (44.2 percent), while Apple has the largest smartphone market share in the United States (28.6 percent). The Windows, BlackBerry, SymbianOS, and Palm/HP webOS operating systems comprise the remaining majority of smartphone market share (**Figure 1**). All of these platforms/operating systems are supported by the jQuery Mobile framework.

MAJOR PLATFORMS

The following list provides a bit more information on the major platforms that are fully supported by the jQuery Mobile framework.

IOS

iOS is Apple's mobile operating system. Originally developed for the iPhone, it has been extended to support other Apple devices such as the iPod Touch, iPad, and Apple TV. iOS uses Safari as its web browser.

ANDROID

Android is an open-source software project and operating system led by Google. It has been used in a plethora of phones, tablets, and other devices since its release under the Apache license. Android uses Google Chrome as its web browser.

WINDOWS PHONE

Windows Phone is Microsoft's mobile operating system. The system is integrated with third-party and other Microsoft services. Windows Phone uses Internet Explorer Mobile as its web browser.

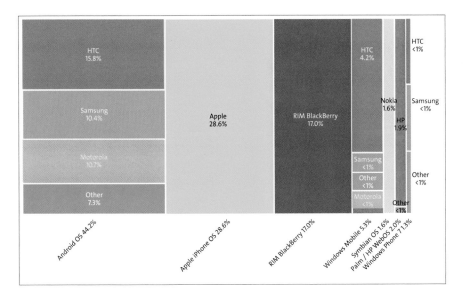

FIGURE 1 Operating system market share as of 2011.

BLACKBERRY

BlackBerry is powered by a proprietary mobile operating system, offered on its own set of smartphones and tablets.

WEBOS

webOS is the open-source operating system used by Palm devices. webOS uses the WebKit layout engine in its web browser, simply named Web.

GRADED SUPPORT

jQuery Mobile uses a three-tier, graded list of the platforms that are supported by the framework. The tiers are A, B, and C. A includes a full experience with the option of Ajax-based page transitions, B includes the same experience minus the Ajax-based page transitions, and C is a basic, yet functional, HTML experience.

A-grade support includes all the major mobile operating systems that were mentioned previously and more, including Apple iOS, Android, Windows Phone, BlackBerry, Palm/HP webOS, Kindle 3, Kindle Fire, and more. B-grade support includes BlackBerry 5, Opera Mini, and Nokia SymbianOS. C-grade support includes BlackBerry 4, Windows Mobile, and all older smartphones and feature phones. This list is always evolving; to see an up-to-date list, visit jquerymobile.com and check out the supported platforms.

PART I

THE
FOUNDATION OF **jQUERY MOBILE**

1

UNDERSTANDING jQUERY

The jQuery framework is the backbone of the jQuery Mobile framework, so it's helpful to know some of the fundamentals of the jQuery framework before developing jQuery Mobile websites. Although it's not required, understanding jQuery will make using jQuery Mobile even easier than it already is, especially if you're interested in writing any sort of custom functionality.

jQuery is a robust yet lightweight JavaScript library that simplifies JavaScript coding and extends the capabilities of Cascading Style Sheets (CSS). In addition, it eliminates cross-browser compatibility issues and is CSS3 compliant. This means quicker scripting, less testing, and less coding for the different ways that browsers handle certain functionality. The jQuery framework is truly an example of how web development should be: You get what you expect the first time, every time.

GETTING **STARTED**

To get started with jQuery, you first need to download the framework from jquery.com and include it in your webpage, or you can simply reference it via the Google, Microsoft, or jQuery content delivery network (CDN). I recommend and most often reference the library via a CDN because it's faster. A CDN will distribute your content across multiple, geographically dispersed servers, so the user receives the closest available file. Plus, Google and Microsoft both offer versions that support secure socket layers (SSL) via HTTPS, must-haves if you're doing any sort of development under SSL. To include the library via a CDN (we'll use Google as an example), use the script element to include it within the <head> elements or at the end of your webpage.

```
<script type="text/javascript"
    src="https://ajax.googleapis.com/ajax/libs/jquery/1.7.1/
    ⟶ jquery.min.js">
</script>
```

Including JavaScript files within the <head> elements is the traditional approach. However, according to Yahoo!, "80 percent of the end-user response time is on the front-end." Most of that time is spent downloading assets, such as style sheets, images, scripts, and so on. It's obviously important to reduce the number of assets, but it's also becoming more common to include JavaScript at the end of an HTML file. This is because scripts block parallel downloads, meaning that other assets will not download until each script is downloaded individually. To ensure that you're placing your scripts in the correct place, simply include them before the closing </html> tag.

It's also best to use the minified version in production environments, because it's smaller than the source version. In addition, although the packed version is smaller than the minified version, it requires client-side processing time to decompress the file and it's not available in the most recent versions. According to Yahoo!, "In a survey of ten top U.S. websites, minification achieved a 21 percent size reduction."

jQUERY **FUNDAMENTALS**

If you're familiar with writing JavaScript and CSS, then writing your first jQuery script will feel very familiar, yet maybe slightly odd. The jQuery framework is a JavaScript library, meaning that it's built with JavaScript. The fundamentals are the same, as you're essentially still writing JavaScript, it just so happens that you'll be writing in a way that uses the jQuery framework. In other words, while there may be added enhancements to certain fundamentals, the core of JavaScript—variables, functions, conditional statements, and so on—has not changed. So, you'll still be using the var keyword, if and switch statements, and functions, but you'll surely notice a lot of additional enhancements and different ways of writing things, namely accessing HTML elements.

jQuery offers many enhancements to the JavaScript language and, as mentioned, the best part is that it's cross-browser compatible, so you don't have to worry about writing multiple versions of the same script to handle different browsers anymore, which is quite a relief. This is especially useful when working with events, Ajax (discussed later in this chapter), and other functionality that traditionally requires some conditional statements to determine how the browser will interpret the code.

SELECTING HTML ELEMENTS

Rather than continually using document.getElementById() to access HTML elements within your webpage, you can simply use a jQuery selector jquery() or the $() function, which is the shorthand version and the one that I will be using throughout this book. Using the jQuery selector not only gives you fewer characters to type, but also lets you do far more than access elements by id. With jQuery selectors, you can also access an array of HTML elements or access an element or object by name. The jQuery selector wraps an element or set of elements into a jQuery object, allowing you to apply jQuery methods to the object itself. And that's not all: You can even access elements by class name or use CSS selectors such as :first-child, :nth-child, among many others. Here are a few examples:

- To access an element by ID using the jQuery selector, use the #id selector, just as you would with CSS when attaching a class to an element by ID:

  $('#foo');

- To access an element by class name, use the `.class` selector, just as you would when creating a CSS class. If you have multiple elements with the same class name, they will all be selected.

```
$('.foo');
```

- To target a specific element with a class name, add the element name before the class name:

```
$('div.foo');
```

- You can even target a specific element or set of elements using an element selector:

```
$('div');
```

If you're familiar with CSS, you're probably starting to see the pattern unfold and the endless possibilities. The options available for structuring a CSS class are the same ones you can use to access an HTML element with the jQuery selector. This is how jQuery enhances JavaScript and CSS, taking the two and merging their syntax into a new language that enhances the overall user experience, when properly used, of course.

MANAGING EVENTS AND FUNCTIONS

Events are used by jQuery to react to user interactions on your webpage, such as mouse clicks. Events are very easy to manage in jQuery, and they're reliable across all the major browsers, which is a big deal, because this isn't always the case with traditional JavaScript. jQuery gives you the ability to intercept many different events from any existing HTML element. Typically, events are used to perform some sort of function. In the following example, a `click` event is bound to a `div` element with foo as the class name:

```
$('div.foo').click(function(e) {
    // Your custom code here
});
```

By binding the click event to the div, a function is associated with clicking the mouse on that particular div. Therefore, anytime div.foo is clicked, your custom code in the handler function will be executed.

If you're familiar with traditional JavaScript, this syntax probably looks strange. Don't worry—it did to me as well when I first started using it, but once I caught on, I liked it. Once you're familiar with it, you'll see that this code syntax is well contained, easy to understand, and easy to write. Let's break down the previous example:

1. The jQuery selector is used to select div.foo, which then becomes a jQuery object.

2. The div.foo jQuery object then uses the click method to fire a handler function when div.foo is clicked.

3. The handler function is used to execute the custom code. The handler also has access to the eventObject, which is passed as an argument. In this example, it is the e argument in the handler function.

If you use the jQuery selector to select a class name that's being used by multiple HTML elements and assign a mouse event, that mouse event will be bound to all of those elements automatically. Therefore, in the example above, if you had multiple div elements with foo as the class name, the click event would be bound to all of them. When working with events that are bound to multiple elements, it's important to consider scope to ensure that any custom code you're executing is applied to the desired element.

```
$('div.foo').click(function(e) {
    alert($(this).html());
});
```

In this example, $(this) is used to access the current element in scope.

> **NOTE:** Scope is the enclosing context that values are associated with. In this case, the function is the enclosing context and $(this) is the value.

$(this) is the same as using the this keyword in JavaScript; in this case, it applies to the element that is currently firing the click event. When considering scope, this always refers to the object associated with the enclosing context. In the example, div.foo is the object and the handler function for the click event is the enclosing context. jQuery will automatically assign the element that is clicked as $(this) inside your anonymous handler function. This lets you access the element that executed the event, even when the same code is applied to multiple elements. Functions are used to execute a script or a set of scripts as the result of an event or a simple and direct call to the function.

As you'll learn later in this book, the bind method is often used by the jQuery Mobile framework to handle custom events.

The custom events provided by jQuery Mobile create useful hooks for development beyond the native functionality of the framework, meaning that you can intercept certain existing events and add your own custom code. Such events include touch, mouse, and window events, all of which you'll learn how to extend later in this book. The syntax for the bind method in jQuery is very similar to the previous code example.

```
$('div.foo').bind('click', function(e) {
    // Your custom code here
});
```

The difference is that you can react to multiple events with the same handler:

```
$('div.foo').bind('mouseenter mouseleave', function(e) {
    // Your custom code here
});
```

NOTE: The difference between a function and a method is that a function is stand-alone and a method is associated with an object. In this case, the bind method is associated with the jQuery object.

Or you can handle custom events, such as those implemented by the jQuery Mobile framework:

```
$('div.foo').bind('displayMyName', function(e, myName) {
    alert('My name is: '+ myName);
});
$('button').click(function () {
    $('div.foo').trigger('displayMyName', ['John Smith']);
});
```

Binding events will be covered in greater depth when we discuss how to bind jQuery Mobile events with custom handler functions.

WAITING FOR DOCUMENTS TO BE READY

A common practice among developers is to wait for a webpage to load before executing any JavaScript. The reason for doing this is to ensure that the webpage elements are available before trying to access or manipulate them. Attempting to access unavailable document elements can lead to unexpected behavior and potentially break all your subsequent JavaScript. With traditional JavaScript, the most common way to wait for the page to load is to use the window.onload event. However, this approach happens after the document loads, because it actually waits for all images and banners to load within a webpage, which can delay your scripts tremendously. Luckily, jQuery provides a ready event that lets your code respond immediately when the document becomes available.

```
$(document).ready(function() {
    // Your custom code here
});
```

First, you need to select the document object itself and then apply the ready event. When the ready event fires, it will execute a function that will contain your custom code. Continuing with the previous examples, you need to add the custom code to the ready event to ensure that the document is ready before trying to apply the click event:

```
$(document).ready(function() {
    $('div.foo').click(function() {
        alert($(this).html());
    });
});
```

Or you can use a shortcut version, which eliminates the need to access the document and set the ready event.

```
$(function() {
    $('div.foo').click(function() {
        alert($(this).html());
    });
});
```

Using the ready event is the de facto standard with any jQuery development. Not only does this approach ensure that your code will fire at the appropriate time, it also lends itself to creating completely unobtrusive code, meaning that you can write all your jQuery in a separate, external file that is simply referenced from your HTML webpage.

APPLYING SPECIAL EFFECTS

jQuery is well-known for the special effects it lets you create without using third-party plug-ins, such as Flash. The library provides many techniques for incorporating animation into a webpage. Animations can create a more visually appealing webpage, or they can serve other, more practical purposes, such as providing visual feedback to user interactions. Many prebuilt animation methods are included in the jQuery framework, such as fadeIn, fadeOut, fadeTo, show, toggle, slideUp, and slideDown, among others.

```
$(document).ready(function() {
    $('div.foo').fadeIn();
});
```

Although these prebuilt animation methods appear to be independent, many of them are powered internally by the animate method. The animate method can be used to animate any numerical CSS property for an HTML element, such as height, opacity, left, and right.

```
$(document).ready(function() {
    $('div.foo').click(function() {
        $(this).animate(function(){
            height: '+=50'
    }, 1000, function() {
            // Your custom code, when the animation is complete
        });
    });
});
```

In this example, when div.foo is clicked, its height property is increased by 50 pixels over a time period of 1 second (1000 milliseconds), and when the animation is complete, a callback function will execute your custom code. A callback function is used to delay the execution of code until something else happens. This is pretty powerful stuff; not only can you animate when an event is fired, you can fire a function or even another event when the animation is complete, and so on.

These examples covered only the animation methods themselves. jQuery includes methods for creating queues to provide additional animation-related functionality. **Table 1.1** lists the queue methods available in jQuery.

TABLE 1.1 Queue methods

METHOD	DESCRIPTION
queue	Queues a string of sequential effects
dequeue	Executes the next function in the queue for specified elements
clearQueue	Removes not-yet-executed items from the queue
delay	Delays the execution of subsequent items in the queue

The queue method provides a way to queue a string of sequential effects, meaning that you can run multiple effects in a queue infinitely or you can stop the queue by using the clearQueue method. The queue method is used primarily by the FX ("effects") queue, which is the default queue, but is also made available via the jQuery API. This lets you queue any functionality that you need to happen sequentially, not solely animations.

The queue and dequeue methods are meant to be associated with a particular element or object. To use the queue method, you need to assign a queueName as the argument, such as an anonymous function:

```
$(document).ready(function() {
    $('div.foo').fadeOut().queue(function(){
        $('div.foo').fadeIn();
        next();
    });
});
```

This sort of functionality lets you produce timeline-based animations without using JavaScript functions such as setTimeout or setInterval.

As mentioned, although queues are often used for effects and are listed under effects in the jQuery documentation, they can also be used to queue other sorts of functionality, such as a series of asynchronous method calls, which leads us to Ajax using jQuery.

USING AJAX

Ajax is an acronym for asynchronous JavaScript and XML. Asynchronous means that you can make a request to a server via Hypertext Transfer Protocol (HTTP) and continue to process other data while waiting for the response. For example, you can make calls to a server-side script to retrieve data from a database as XML, send data to a server-side script to be stored in a database, or simply load an XML file to populate pages of your website without refreshing the webpage. The functionality available through the jQuery framework makes Ajax development much easier than traditional JavaScript, by requiring less code and offering additional methods and event handlers to cover any situation. The amount of jQuery code needed to handle Ajax is minimal compared to traditional JavaScript, even when developing complex functionality, which ultimately makes development much faster.

With traditional JavaScript, Ajax requires a lot of redundant code to form a request and handle the response because of all the variations that are necessary for the different browsers. To make a request and handle the response, you need to write code similar to the following:

```
if(window.XMLHttpRequest) {
    request = new XMLHttpRequest();
}
else if(window.ActiveXObject) {
    request = new ActiveXObject('MSXML2.XMLHTTP');
}
request.onreadystatechange = onResponse;
request.open('GET', 'url for request', true);
request.send(null);
function checkReadyState(obj) {
    if(obj.readyState == 0) { // Sending Request }
    if(obj.readyState == 1) { // Loading Response }
    if(obj.readyState == 2) { // Response Loaded }
    if(obj.readyState == 3) { // Response Ready }
    if(obj.readyState == 4) {
        if(obj.status == 200) {
            return true;
        }
        else if(obj.status == 404) {
            // File not found
        }
        else {
            // There was a problem retrieving the XML
        }
    }
```

```
    }
    function onResponse() {
        if(checkReadyState(request)) {
            // Handle the response with one of the following properties
            //alert(request.responseXML);
            //alert(request.responseText);
        }
    }
```

jQuery is accomplishing the same functionality as traditional JavaScript, but you don't have to worry about writing most of it. It's not that traditional JavaScript is hard to write; it's just that there's a lot to write and it tends to get messy, especially when you compare it to how easy it is to write a request and response with jQuery. The following is a sample Ajax request using jQuery, which is very similar to the previous JavaScript example:

```
jQuery.ajax({
    url: 'url for request',
    success: function(xml) {
        // Parse the response
    }
});
```

This code uses the jQuery object's ajax method, includes a url property for the request, and handles a success callback with an anonymous function. Many more properties can be used within the jQuery object's ajax method, such as the type of request, either POST or GET (the default), a username and password, and crossDomain. However, this example shows the ajax method in its most basic form to illustrate the simplicity of jQuery Ajax calls.

Ajax is used in the jQuery Mobile framework to handle page changes and to load or preload a page. The framework provides access through the application programming interface (API) to handle this functionality, and we'll cover it in-depth later in this book.

WRAPPING **UP**

jQuery has made user-interface enhancements far easier by simplifying JavaScript and combining it with the syntax of CSS. The framework provides a way to write less, spend less time testing, and achieve more complex results in less time. jQuery lets you enhance webpages by easily adding custom interactions, as well as custom effects to provide visual feedback to users, ultimately creating a better user experience.

This book is not intended to teach the jQuery framework, but this chapter reviewed concepts that are necessary to understand and work with the jQuery Mobile framework. To learn more about the jQuery framework, visit jquery.com. The online documentation is very comprehensive and includes code samples, developer comments, and in-depth descriptions of the available objects, methods, events, and so on. You can also visit the jQuery forums at forum.jquery.com, where other developers are available to help with any coding questions you may have.

2

THE **ROLE** OF **HTML5**

As the starting point for all jQuery Mobile development, HTML5 plays a key role in the jQuery Mobile framework. HTML5 provides the gateway for everything from defining how your webpage renders in mobile, tablet, or desktop browsers to custom attributes that define widgets and themes and much more. This chapter provides an overview of how HTML5 is used and what features are utilized most by the jQuery Mobile framework.

SEMANTIC HTML5

Accessibility is a major focus and priority of the jQuery Mobile framework. This is one reason why the framework is built on semantic HTML and why it's available to the widest possible range of devices. The techniques that the framework uses to support A-grade browsers even provide access for users with screen readers such as VoiceOver for Apple iPhone.

jQuery Mobile uses three levels to grade the support of the framework: A, B, and C. A is full; B is full, minus Ajax; and C is basic support.

Standard, semantic HTML gives you the security of providing a mobile website that is accessible to the greatest range of users without having to do the testing yourself. This is the power of the jQuery Mobile framework.

CREATING AN HTML5 TEMPLATE

Creating a basic page template using HTML5 is incredibly easy. All you need to do is add the `<!DOCTYPE>` declaration followed by standard HTML, such as opening and closing `html`, `head`, `title`, and `body` elements. The declaration must be the first thing in your HTML5 document because it instructs the browser about what version of HTML is being used so it can interpret your markup.

```
<!DOCTYPE html>
<html>
    <head>
        <title>Page Title</title>
    </head>
<body>
</body>
</html>
```

The `<!DOCTYPE>` declaration is supported by all major browsers. It's also much simpler to use than previous versions of HTML. HTML 4, for example, includes three different versions of the `<!DOCTYPE>` declaration and requires the document type definition (DTD) because it's based on Standard Generalized Markup Language (SGML).

THE **VIEWPORT** META **TAG**

FIGURE 2.1 A website without the viewport association that best accommodates mobile devices.

The `viewport` meta tag was introduced by mobile Safari to let web developers control the size and scale of the viewport. Many other major mobile browsers now support this tag. It is used to set the browser's layout viewport to improve the presentation of webpages. Mobile web browsers obviously have a much smaller screen size than desktop browsers and because of this they have a different layout viewport association. If you've ever viewed a desktop website on a mobile phone that isn't using a viewport association that accommodates mobile devices, you've most likely noticed that the site looks similar to Figure 2.1. Without the `viewport` tag, your webpage can appear small, or zoomed out, as any other webpage not built for mobile would display. The webpage can be very hard to read without zooming in.

NOTE: The iPhone screenshot used for Figure 2.1 was captured in Mobilizer, a mobile preview tool from Springbox (http://www.springbox.com/mobilizer/).

You can include the `viewport` meta tag in a separate mobile website that accommodates the smaller browser display, but this is often beyond many companies' capabilities, because it adds time and cost. Plus, the management of two separate websites is often too much to handle. Currently, the standard option for rendering your website properly is to use the `viewport` meta tag. This tag tells the browser to optimize your website based on the best width for viewing it in that browser. To use the `viewport` meta tag to set the display, set the name of the meta tag to `viewport`, then use the `content` attribute to set properties and values that meet your needs. Within the `content` attribute, you can define the properties and values you want to set for the layout. To add multiple properties to a `viewport` meta tag, you need to create a comma-delimited list of property and value sets. Here's the most common setup for the `viewport` meta tag in mobile development:

```
<meta name="viewport" content="width=device-width, initial-scale=1">
```

To include this tag in your HTML5 template, add it within the head element:

```
<!DOCTYPE html>

<html>

    <head>

        <meta http-equiv="Content-Type" content="text/html;
        → charset=UTF-8">

        <meta name="viewport" content="width=device-width,
        → initial-scale=1">

        <title>Page Title</title>

    </head>

<body>

</body>

</html>
```

The most important property to set is the `width`, which should be set to `device-width` for mobile websites. The second property is `initial-scale`, which defines the state of the website when it first loads, after which users can zoom in or out. For example, if you were to set the `initial-scale` to 2, rather than 1, by default the website would be scaled by 2 (that is, 2 would be used as the multiplier for scaling). **Table 2.1** describes these and other meta `viewport` properties in more detail.

TABLE 2.1 Meta viewport properties

PROPERTY	DESCRIPTION
width	Sets the width of the viewport in pixels. The value can be a specific number in pixels; the default is 980. You can also use a dynamic value, such as the width of the device (device-width). The device-width value is commonly used in mobile development, because it dynamically sets the width of the viewport to the width of the device, and therefore accommodates all scenarios.
height	Sets the height of the viewport in pixels. The value can be a specific number in pixels.
initial-scale	Defines the scale of the website when it initially loads. The value should be a number or decimal. The value is the multiplier by which the initial scale is set.
minimum-scale	Defines the minimum scale of the website. The default is .25, and the range is >0 to 10.
maximum-scale	Defines the maximum scale of the website. The default is 1.6, and the range is >0 to 10.
user-scalable	Determines whether or not the user can zoom in and out to change the scale of the viewport. A value of yes allows scaling, while a value of no restricts scaling. A value of no also prevents a webpage from scrolling when entering text into a form field.

When designing or developing for mobile websites, it's important to understand how your content will display on different devices. Remember that handheld devices come in many shapes and sizes and that there are both portrait and landscape modes to contend with. I always consider using CSS and/or `viewport` properties to create scalable layouts. However, by using the `viewport` meta tag code from the code example along with the jQuery Mobile framework, you can be assured that your website will render as accurately as possible on a wide range of devices.

UNDERSTANDING
DATA- ATTRIBUTES

HTML5 data- attributes let you store custom data that's unseen by the user. In other words, the data is not rendered or even used by the browser. With previous versions of HTML, custom data is often stored in title, rel, class, or id attributes, or in hidden HTML elements. The data stored in these attributes is accessible to JavaScript. There are many reasons why access to custom data is useful via JavaScript; it can be used behind the scenes to create custom functionality or displayed to the user when a specific interaction occurs. A good example of using custom data in a webpage is in an image gallery: A title and a description can be added to an image and then used by JavaScript to display information about the image that the user is viewing. The bottom line is that this is a misuse of these HTML attributes, but until now it has been the only way to handle certain functionality that is otherwise unsupported. Luckily, developers can start using HTML attributes appropriately with the support of data- attributes.

Rather than having to use attributes with other predetermined uses, you can now create custom data- attributes that are more relevant to your data and still render valid HTML. The HTML5 specification supports any attribute that begins with data- as a data storage area. Any name you want to append to the data- prefix will be supported. For example, if you add custom data- attributes to an image tag that belongs to an image gallery, you can add custom data-title and data-description attributes and give them any custom value.

```
<img src="image-path/img.jpg" data-title="My image title"
→ data-description="My image description">
```

NOTE: The only restrictions on creating custom data- attributes are that the custom portion of the attribute must be at least one character long and cannot contain uppercase letters.

The attribute value can be any string, and as always, you need to escape any double quotes within your strings.

Keep in mind the possibility of potential name clashing. As data- attributes become more widespread, it's likely that JavaScript libraries will be looking for attributes with similar names, especially if generic attribute names are used, such as data-description. A good solution to this problem is to use a custom namespace within the name of the data- attribute. For example, if you're developing a website for jquerymobile.tv, you could use jquerymobiletv as your namespace in the data- attribute:

data-jquerymobiletv-foo

Not only does this prevent potential name clashing, it also personalizes the code and makes it specific to your website or application.

The jQuery Mobile framework uses a number of custom data- attributes for widgets and theming. These attributes are used during initialization and configuration. Two common data- attributes are listed in Table 2.2.

TABLE 2.2 Common data- attributes in jQuery Mobile

data- ATTRIBUTE	DESCRIPTION
data-role	Used to define any of the widgets in the jQuery Mobile framework. Setting this attribute within an HTML element lets you add a widget to your webpage automatically.
data-theme	Used by the jQuery Mobile framework to define how your widgets should look. This attribute sets the theme for a widget using jQuery Mobile.

Later in this book we'll take an in-depth look at theming and using data-theme attributes with jQuery Mobile. We'll also cover more data- attributes associated with the various widgets provided by the framework.

The framework itself allows you to define a custom namespace using a global option in the configuration called *ns* (namespace). The ns option can be set to any custom value, such as jquerymobiletv-. If you do use a custom namespace, it's best to use a dash at the end:

data-jquerymobiletv-foo

Otherwise, the result won't include a dash between your namespace and the custom data- value, so your data- attributes will be hard to read, and jQuery Mobile will look for an attribute that looks like the following example:

data-jquerymobiletvfoo

Be aware that choosing a custom namespace requires you to commit to that namespace during coding. For example, when defining a jQuery Mobile header you would normally use:

```
data-role="header"
```

To add this attribute to your HTML5 template you could simply add a `div` that includes the attribute:

```
<!DOCTYPE html>
<html>
    <head>
        <title>Page Title</title>
        <meta name="viewport" content="width=device-width,
        → initial-scale=1">
    </head>
<body>
    <div data-role="header">
        <h1>Header</h1>
    </div>
</body>
</html>
```

However, if you define a custom namespace in the configuration, you'll need to define your header as:

```
data-jquerymobiletv-role="header"
```

We'll talk about configuration options, including the `ns` option, in more detail later in the book.

With the introduction of `data-` attributes, developers have much more control over the data that is added to a webpage. Custom attributes provide a means to support semantic HTML while enhancing the webpage with front-end scripting languages, such as JavaScript.

WRAPPING **UP**

It may be daunting to think that you need to understand HTML5 and jQuery to use the jQuery Mobile framework. Thankfully, the framework is built in a way that supports developers with different skill levels. You don't necessarily have to know HTML5 and jQuery, because the framework provides a template for HTML5 that you can download directly from jquerymobile.com, and jQuery is available to those developers who want to use it. The only thing that's absolutely necessary is to understand how to use data- attributes, because this is the way to add widgets to a webpage without using jQuery.

3

GETTING STARTED WITH **JQUERY MOBILE**

In the previous chapters, we covered basic jQuery, how to create an HTML5 template, how to add a `viewport` meta tag for mobile browsing, and how to use `data-` attributes. Now you're ready to dive into jQuery Mobile and see how these languages, elements, and attributes are leveraged and enhanced using the framework. One of the great things about the jQuery Mobile framework is that at its core it's basic HTML5 markup and JavaScript, which is supported by all major browsers. For basic jQuery Mobile development, there honestly isn't that much to learn. This chapter covers the few steps and provides a little background as to what's happening behind the scenes. In later chapters, you'll see how you can expand on these basic concepts to create more advanced jQuery Mobile websites and even mobile web applications.

HOW jQUERY MOBILE WORKS

There are many ways to build a jQuery Mobile website. However, in its simplest form, the framework functions on top of HTML5 and the jQuery library to transform elements with data- attributes into components, making it very easy to incorporate into your existing web development practices. The most basic components of the framework are pages and toolbars, which will be explained in more detail later in this chapter. But first, let's look at how to incorporate the jQuery Mobile framework into an HTML5 webpage.

ADDING THE jQUERY MOBILE FRAMEWORK TO YOUR WEBSITE

For starters, the jQuery Mobile framework is available at jquerymobile.com. There are two ways to add the jQuery Mobile framework to your webpages.

The first way is to download individual packages, which include both full and minified versions of the JavaScript library and CSS file. You will also need to download the jQuery library from jquery.com.

The second (and recommended) option is to include a direct reference to the CDN-hosted files as seen here:

```
<link rel="stylesheet" href="http://code.jquery.com/mobile/1.0/
    jquery.mobile-1.0.min.css" />
```

```
<script src="http://ajax.googleapis.com/ajax/libs/jquery/1.7.1/
    jquery.min.js"></script>
```

```
<script src="http://code.jquery.com/mobile/1.0/jquery.
    mobile-1.0.min.js"></script>
```

NOTE: Keep in mind that at the time this book was written the latest version of the jQuery Mobile framework was final version 1. To get the latest code for including these files, visit jquerymobile.com, where you can simply copy and paste it into your webpages.

To add the framework to the HTML5 template you created in Chapter 2, "The Role of HTML5," add it within the head element:

```
<!DOCTYPE html>
<html>
    <head>
        <meta http-equiv="Content-Type" content="text/html;
        → charset=UTF-8">

        <meta name="viewport" content="width=device-width,
        → initial-scale=1">

        <title>Page Title</title>

        <link rel="stylesheet" href="http://code.jquery.com/
        → mobile/1.0/jquery.mobile-1.0.min.css" />

        <script src="http://ajax.googleapis.com/ajax/libs/
        → jquery/1.7.1/jquery.min.js"></script>

        <script src="http://code.jquery.com/mobile/1.0/
        → jquery.mobile-1.0.min.js"></script>

    </head>
<body>
</body>
</html>
```

The primary reason that content delivery network (CDN)-hosted files are recommended is because the load time is faster. A CDN will distribute your content across multiple, geographically dispersed servers, so the user who is accessing your webpage receives the closest available web files.

If you're developing Microsoft .net applications, you can use the Microsoft CDN-hosted jQuery Mobile files, which are currently available at http://www.asp.net/ajaxLibrary/CDNjQueryMobile10.ashx.

With the jQuery Mobile framework in place, you can begin to transform your HTML5 markup into rich mobile components. Let's take a look at the most common components: pages and toolbars.

PAGE AND TOOLBAR COMPONENTS

In jQuery Mobile, a page is literally defined by an HTML element with a data-role attribute set to a value of page:

```
<div data-role="page"></div>
```

Voilà. I'm not sure if it can get any easier than this. jQuery Mobile will convert this <div> element (most commonly used) into a page component. All you need to do is use this markup and embed the framework in the <head> of your webpage.

Within the data-role="page" element, you can use whatever HTML markup you prefer. The most common elements to see within a data-role="page" element are <div> elements with data-role attribute values of header, content, and footer. The header and footer data-role attributes are both considered toolbar components in jQuery Mobile, while the content data-role is simply used to define the content area of your website in which you can add any HTML markup. The following example shows a typical HTML structure for a basic jQuery Mobile webpage using these data-roles:

```
<!DOCTYPE HTML>
<html>
    <head>
        <meta http-equiv="Content-Type" content="text/html;
        → charset=UTF-8">

        <meta name="viewport" content="width=device-width,
        → initial-scale=1">

        <title>Basic template - jQuery Mobile: Design and Develop
        → </title>

        <link rel="stylesheet" href="http://code.jquery.com/
        → mobile/1.0/jquery.mobile-1.0.min.css" />

        <script src="http://ajax.googleapis.com/ajax/libs/
        → jquery/1.7.1/jquery.min.js"></script>

        <script src="http://code.jquery.com/mobile/1.0/
        → jquery.mobile-1.0.min.js"></script>
    </head>
```

```
<body>
    <div data-role="page">
        <div data-role="header">
            <h1>Page title</h1>
        </div>
        <div data-role="content">
            Body copy
        </div>
        <div data-role="footer">
            Copyright
        </div>
    </div>
</body>
</html>
```

FIGURE 3.1 jQuery Mobile visually transforms markup with specific **data-** attributes.

The code looks very similar to our previous examples, with the addition of the page, header, content, and footer elements. The visual transformation of this markup by jQuery Mobile can be seen in **Figure 3.1**.

The header, content, and footer are all transformed into a basic layout that visually separates each of the sections. This is the default jQuery Mobile theme; later in this book you'll learn how to create custom themes. In this example, the page title is displayed prominently at the top within the header, while the body copy is formatted using the content data- attribute and the copyright is displayed in a defined footer area.

STRUCTURING MOBILE WEBPAGES

There are two ways to structure webpages for jQuery Mobile. The first is to incorporate all the pages within the same file; the second is to create separate files, like a typical website. To create multiple pages within a single HTML file, you can delineate multiple page data-roles, which allows each page data-role to contain its own header, content, footer, and so on. The following example gives you a basic idea of how to create a multipage jQuery Mobile website in a single HTML file:

```
<!DOCTYPE html>
<html>
    <head>
        <meta http-equiv="Content-Type" content="text/html;
        ⇢ charset=UTF-8">
        <meta name="viewport" content="width=device-width,
        ⇢ initial-scale=1">
        <title>Page Title</title>
        <link rel="stylesheet" href="http://code.jquery.com/
        ⇢ mobile/1.0/jquery.mobile-1.0.min.css" />
        <script src="http://ajax.googleapis.com/ajax/libs/
        ⇢ jquery/1.7.1/jquery.min.js"></script>
        <script src="http://code.jquery.com/mobile/1.0/
        ⇢ jquery.mobile-1.0.min.js"></script>
    </head>
<body>
    <div data-role="page" id="page-one">
        <div data-role="header">
            <h1>Page 1</h1>
        </div>
```

```
    <div data-role="content">Body copy for page 1</div>
    <div data-role="footer">Copyright</div>
</div>
<div data-role="page" id="page-two">
    <div data-role="header">
        <h1>Page 2</h1>
    </div>
    <div data-role="content">Body copy for page 2</div>
    <div data-role="footer">Copyright</div>
</div>
</body>
</html>
```

This approach is not recommended, because files structured this way usually become harder to manage and are much larger in file size, so they ultimately will take longer to load. For demos or prototypes, this may be an option, but it is strongly recommended that you build your mobile websites or applications as separate HTML files.

When using separate HTML files for your webpages, the page data-role is used as a container that the framework loads other webpages into. For example, let's say you have two separate HTML files, page-1.html and page-2.html. Then you add the page data-role attribute to both files and hyperlink page-1.html to page-2.html:

```
<!DOCTYPE HTML>
<html>
<head>
    <meta http-equiv="Content-Type" content="text/html;
    → charset=UTF-8">
    <meta name="viewport" content="width=device-width,
    → initial-scale=1">
```

```
<title>Page 1 - jQuery Mobile: Design and Develop</title>
<link rel="stylesheet" href="http://code.jquery.com/mobile/1.0/
 → jquery.mobile-1.0.min.css" />
<script src="http://ajax.googleapis.com/ajax/libs/jquery/1.7.1/
 → jquery.min.js"></script>
<script src="http://code.jquery.com/mobile/1.0/
 → jquery.mobile-1.0.min.js"></script>
</head>
<body>
    <div data-role="page">
        <div data-role="header">
            <h1>Page 1 Title</h1>
        </div>
        <div data-role="content">
            <a href="page-2.html">Link to page 2</a>
        </div>
        <div data-role="footer">
            Copyright
        </div>
    </div>
</body>
</html>
```

With the jQuery Mobile framework included, the page data-role of page-1.html will automatically become the container to load the markup within the page data-role of page-2.html using an XMLHttpRequest. The XMLHttpRequest is what Ajax uses to exchange data with the server without refreshing the webpage;

FIGURE 3.2 jQuery Mobile uses an XMLHttpRequest to load subsequent pages.

it's sort of like a portal to the backend. **Figure 3.2** shows an example of the XMLHttpRequest that is made when page-1.html links to page-2.html. The request was logged using Chrome Developer Tools. Chrome Developer Tools were used in this case to see that the XMLHttpRequest was made by jQuery Mobile when the link to page-2.html was clicked. Chrome Developer Tools provide a great way to test and debug code.

NOTE: Chrome Developer Tools are an integrated web development environment built in to the Chrome browser.

The HTML page itself is requested and jQuery Mobile uses its contents to display the new page. There's a lot to learn about this simple request, and we'll cover it in more detail in the coming chapters.

WRAPPING **UP**

Creating pages and including the jQuery Mobile framework is incredibly easy; the depth of the framework shines through when we uncover the details that make this framework so robust. As you've learned, data- attributes provide a way to store custom data that is unseen by the user, but the data remains accessible to JavaScript and, ultimately, to jQuery. This is why data- attributes play a large role in jQuery Mobile. The framework uses these attributes to transform basic HTML elements that use them as stylized widgets. We've only scratched the surface of pages and toolbars, and there are still many other components to discuss. With this basic information under your belt, it's time to jump in and see what jQuery Mobile has to offer.

PART II

UI
COMPONENTS

4

CREATING MULTIPAGE WEBSITES

Now that we've covered the basics of structuring mobile webpages, we'll take a deeper look and get a better understanding of the functionality behind them. As mentioned in Chapter 3, "Getting Started with jQuery Mobile," there are two ways to structure webpages for jQuery Mobile: incorporate all the pages in the same file, or create separate files for each page like a typical website. Understanding the different page template types is the foundation for customizing a number of different page-related functionalities. In addition to learning about the page template types, you'll also see how to preload and cache pages, work with different page transitions, and customize loading messages. You'll learn to create custom functionality to take your pages to the next level.

MULTIPAGE TEMPLATE

Internal linking occurs automatically when you have multiple jQuery Mobile pages in the same HTML file. As you've learned, jQuery Mobile pages are defined by adding a data-role with a value of page to an HTML element and anything within that page becomes relative to that page. In jQuery Mobile, typical separate webpages are considered *single-page* templates, while webpages that contain multiple pages are considered *multipage* templates. Let's refer back to our multipage template example from the previous chapter (with a few small additions):

```
<!DOCTYPE html>

<html>

    <head>

        <meta http-equiv="Content-Type" content="text/html;
        → charset=UTF-8">

        <meta name="viewport" content="width=device-width,
        → initial-scale=1">

        <title>Multipage template - jQuery Mobile: Design and
        → Develop</title>

        <link rel="stylesheet" href="http://code.jquery.com/
        → mobile/1.0.1/jquery.mobile-1.0.1.min.css" />

        <script src="http://ajax.googleapis.com/ajax/libs/
        → jquery/1.7.1/jquery.min.js"></script>

        <script src="http://code.jquery.com/mobile/1.0.1/
        → jquery.mobile-1.0.1.min.js"></script>

</script>

        <script type="text/javascript" src="assets/js/ui.js">

</script>

    </head>

<body class="container">

    <div data-role="page" id="page-one" data-title="Page 1">

        <div data-role="header">

            <h1>Page 1</h1>

        </div>
```

```
        <div data-role="content">
            <p>Body copy for page 1</p>
            <p><a href="#page-two">Link to page 2</a></p>
        </div>
        <div data-role="footer">
            Copyright
        </div>
    </div>
    <div data-role="page" id="page-two" data-title="Page 2">
        <div data-role="header">
            <h1>Page 2</h1>
        </div>
        <div data-role="content">
            <p>Body copy for page 2</p>
            <a href="#page-one">Link to page 1</a>
        </div>
        <div data-role="footer">
            Copyright
        </div>
    </div>
</body>
</html>
```

Within this multipage template are two pages defined by div elements with custom ids. The jQuery Mobile framework shows only one of these pages at a time, and it uses the data-title attribute to change the page title dynamically. The page that is shown by default is determined by the order of the source code. In this example, the first page has an id of page-one, but if the pages in this file were switched, so that the element with an id of page-two came first, then that would be the default page to load. In other words, the value of the id attribute doesn't

FIGURE 4.1 A multipage
template with two pages and
the transition in between.

determine what page is shown by default; the default page is determined only by
the source code order. However, the id is used for other important purposes, such
as linking pages to one another.

This is where jQuery Mobile pages begin to act like separate webpages. Note
that hyperlinks have been added to the original template to link from one page to
another. This is somewhat like the toggle functionality that's common in JavaScript
development, where id values are used to hide and reveal certain HTML elements.
The difference here is that jQuery Mobile handles the functionality for you. To link
from one page to another you simply need to:

1. Create a hyperlink.
2. Type the pound sign (#).
3. Specify the id value of the page you want to link to.

The end result looks like this:

```
<a href="#page-two">Link to page 2</a>
```

It's similar to creating a page anchor; the difference is that you're referencing
the id value of another page. Remember that each page needs a unique id value.
In this case, I've used page-one and page-two, but you can use something more
descriptive and relative to the content of your jQuery Mobile page. The cool thing
about the jQuery Mobile framework is that it transitions dynamically from one
page to another without requiring you to write an ounce of code. **Figure 4.1** shows
an example of this code in both page views and the transition from one to another.

SINGLE-PAGE TEMPLATE

Single-page templates are separate HTML files that act as independent webpages, just like any standard webpage. The main difference is in how jQuery Mobile connects webpages using Ajax. As with multipage templates, the Ajax-based navigation in single-page templates uses hashtags to create a page history. The Ajax-based navigation used by jQuery Mobile is the default, but it can be turned off by setting the ajaxEnabled setting to false in the configuration. You'll learn more about the configuration settings later in this book.

Ajah is an abbreviation that is sometimes used for Asynchronous JavaScript and HTML. Ajah is essentially Ajax without the XML; the XMLHttpRequest is still used, but HTML is exchanged with the server rather than XML. This is what jQuery Mobile uses as the user browses independent webpages. We briefly covered how the jQuery Mobile framework uses the XMLHttpRequest to load subsequent pages in the previous chapter, but there's a lot to learn and understand about this simple request.

One great thing about the jQuery Mobile framework is how it tracks history: it supports the back and forward buttons! Also, while subsequent pages load, the framework provides a default loading message and transitions between pages. The default page transition is to slide between two pages, and the default loading message is a spinning icon with a "loading..." message. Both options are configurable, as you'll learn in the next chapter. For now, let's see how hashtags and history work in jQuery Mobile.

HASHTAGS AND HISTORY

jQuery Mobile uses hashtags to manage history in single- and multipage templates. The window object's location.hash is used to make changes and updates to the history, so the back and forward buttons function as usual, which is uncommon in other Ajax-based systems. Essentially, jQuery Mobile prevents the default functionality of all hyperlinks and uses the hashtag functionality to handle history. Not only is the history updated, the hashtag system also creates a valid URL that can be bookmarked for later reference.

The only issue with jQuery Mobile's hashtag-based navigation is that it doesn't support deep linking. However, there are some workarounds you can use to support this functionality. With a little help from jQuery, you can add a script, like the following, to your webpage and your deep links will function as usual:

```
$(document).ready(function() {
    $('a[href^="#"]').bind('click vclick', function () {
        location.hash = $(this).attr('href');
        return false;
    });
});
```

In HTML, all hyperlinks that include a pound sign (#) as their first character are identified as anchors. This script uses a regular expression that includes the caret symbol to identify all anchor elements that have an href attribute with a value that begins with the pound sign. Once these elements have been selected, you can use the bind method to bind a click and vclick event to the anchor tags and assign an anonymous function handler as the callback.

The callback function sets the window object's location.hash to the value of the anchor and returns false to prevent the browser from performing the default action associated with clicking the hyperlink.

NOTES: The caret (^) symbol is often used in regular expressions to designate the beginning of a string.

The vclick event is an option used in jQuery Mobile by devices that support touch events. The event supports faster page changes and during page transitions it keeps the address bar hidden.

Hyperlinking from single-page to multipage templates with Ajax enabled will load only the first page in the source code of the multipage template. To link to a multipage template from a single-page template, you must use an external hyperlink by using rel="external" or data-ajax="false".

LINK TYPES

jQuery Mobile supports standard HTML link types as well as a number of custom link types related to the mobile experience. The following tables offer a list of the supported link types available through the jQuery Mobile framework. Each table shows options categorized based on their end result and/or support of Ajax. **Table 4.1** describes links that support Ajax.

TABLE 4.1 Link types that support Ajax

HYPERLINK MARKUP	DESCRIPTION
`<a href="http://www.jquerymobile.tv">` `Hyperlink within same domain </a>`	A standard HTML link that is transformed by the jQuery Mobile framework to use Ajax, include page transitions, and support page history.
`<a href="http://www.jquerymobile.tv"` `data-rel="dialog"> Open a dialog</a>`	An option used for dialog windows that is not tracked in page history.
`<a href="http://www.jquerymobile.tv"` `data-rel="back">Back button</a>`	This option can be used to navigate back in page history; it's a great option for providing a back button from a page or dialog. The href is ignored in A- and B-grade browsers, but is necessary for C-grade browsers.

GRADED SUPPORT

As mentioned in the book's introduction, jQuery Mobile uses a three-tier graded list of platforms that are supported by the framework: A, B, and C. A includes a full experience with the option of Ajax-based page transitions; B includes the same experience minus the Ajax-based page transitions; and C is a basic yet functional HTML experience.

A-grade support includes all the major mobile operating systems mentioned previously and others, including Apple iOS, Android, Windows Phone, BlackBerry, Palm WebOS, Kindle 3, and Kindle Fire. B-grade support includes BlackBerry 5, Opera Mini, and Nokia Symbian. C-grade support includes BlackBerry 4, Windows Mobile, and all older smartphones and feature phones. Visit jquerymobile.com to see an up-to-date list of supported platforms.

Table 4.2 describes a list of hyperlinks that disable the Ajax page-transition functionality. These hyperlinks are great for pages on an external domain, pages that open in a new window, linking from single to multipage templates, or linking to pages where you don't want to use Ajax.

Table 4.3 includes link types that stem from a basic HTML hyperlink with the addition of specific attributes.

TABLE 4.2 Link types that disable Ajax

HYPERLINK MARKUP	DESCRIPTION
`<a href="http://www.jquery.com">External` `→ hyperlink</a>`	Linking to a page on an external domain automatically disables the Ajax functionality.
`<a href="http://www.jquery.com" rel="external">` `→ External hyperlink</a>`	By default this attribute defines a hyperlink as external, which not only disables Ajax, but also removes it from the page hashtag history and refreshes the webpage. This option can be transformed using jQuery to open new windows in a standards-compliant way.
`<a href="http://www.jquery.com"` `→ data-ajax="false">Hyperlink disables Ajax</a>`	This option provides a way to define a hyperlink as external, which not only disables Ajax, but also removes it from the page hashtag history and refreshes the webpage.

TABLE 4.3 Miscellaneous link types

HYPERLINK MARKUP	DESCRIPTION
`<a href="tel:15556667777">Phone Number</a>`	This hyperlink initiates a phone call when clicked on some phones.
`<a href="mailto:jdoe@jquerymobile.tv">` `→ Email link</a>`	This hyperlink initiates a new email that's prefilled with the specified email address.
`<a href="#">Hyperlink</a>`	This hyperlink returns false. It's useful when creating a back button as in Table 4.1.

The jQuery Mobile framework uses many hyperlink attributes to create enhancements to otherwise normal HTML webpages. This is just another reason why jQuery Mobile is more appealing than creating a mobile website from scratch. It lets you focus on what matters, eliminating the need to write core functionality every time you create a new mobile website.

The following examples show a few of the link types covered in the tables.

This webpage offers three examples of the link types that can be used in jQuery Mobile: an internal link, an external link, and a link that disables Ajax:

```html
<!DOCTYPE html>
<html>
    <head>
        <meta http-equiv="Content-Type" content="text/html;
        ⇢ charset=UTF-8">
        <meta name="viewport" content="width=device-width,
        ⇢ initial-scale=1">
        <title>Single-page template - Page 1 - jQuery Mobile: Design
        ⇢ and Develop</title>
        <link rel="stylesheet" href="http://code.jquery.com/
        ⇢ mobile/1.0.1/jquery.mobile-1.0.1.min.css" />
        <script src="http://ajax.googleapis.com/ajax/libs/
        ⇢ jquery/1.7.1/jquery.min.js"></script>
        <script src="http://code.jquery.com/mobile/1.0.1/
        ⇢ jquery.mobile-1.0.1.min.js"></script>
        </script>
    </head>
<body class="container">
    <div data-role="page">
        <div data-role="header">
            <h1>Page 1</h1>
        </div>
        <div data-role="content">
            <p><a href="single-page-2.html">Link to page 2</a></p>
            <p><a href="single-page-2.html" rel="external">
            ⇢ External Link to page 2</a></p>
            <p><a href="single-page-2.html" data-ajax="false">
            ⇢ Ajax-disabled link to page 2</a></p>
```

```
        </div>
        <div data-role="footer">
            Copyright
        </div>
    </div>
</body>
</html>
```

An internal link requires no special markup and is where the framework will interject and create a page transition between the current page and the page that's being linked to. An external link is one that requires the rel attribute, which must be set to a value of external. Setting a hyperlink as external disables Ajax, removes it from the page hashtag history, and refreshes the webpage when the link is clicked. The link that disables Ajax requires a data-ajax attribute with a value of false. This disables Ajax, removes it from the page hashtag history, and refreshes the webpage, just like the previous example, with the main difference being that the rel="external" attribute can be used as a standards-compliant way to create hyperlinks that target new windows with a little help from jQuery.

In this next example, there's an internal link and a hyperlink that acts as a back button:

```
<!DOCTYPE html>
<html>
    <head>
        <meta http-equiv="Content-Type" content="text/html;
        → charset=UTF-8">
        <meta name="viewport" content="width=device-width,
        → initial-scale=1">
        <title>Single-page template - Page 2 - jQuery Mobile: Design
        → and Develop</title>
        <link rel="stylesheet" href="http://code.jquery.com/
        → mobile/1.0.1/jquery.mobile-1.0.1.min.css" />
```

```
        <script src="http://ajax.googleapis.com/ajax/libs/
    →   jquery/1.7.1/jquery.min.js"></script>
        <script src="http://code.jquery.com/mobile/1.0.1/
    →   jquery.mobile-1.0.1.min.js"></script>
    </head>
<body class="container">
    <div data-role="page">
        <div data-role="header">
            <h1>Page 2</h1>
        </div>
        <div data-role="content">
            <p><a href="single-page.html">Ajax link to page 1</a></p>
            <p><a href="#" data-rel="back">Back button</a></p>
        </div>
        <div data-role="footer">
            Copyright
        </div>
    </div>
</body>
</html>
```

Setting the data-rel attribute to back creates a hyperlink that acts like a back button. When this link is clicked, the jQuery Mobile framework automatically links to the previous page in history.

PRELOADING AND CACHING PAGES

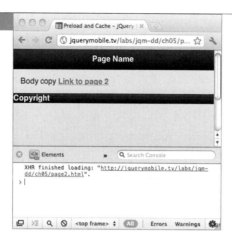

FIGURE 4.2 A page being preloaded by jQuery Mobile using the prefetch attribute.

Page caching is very important when working with anything web-based. Cache refers to hidden storage where files are collected. By default, browsers handle webpage caching by putting the associated files in a local directory on the user's computer so the webpage and its associated assets will load more quickly during subsequent visits. jQuery Mobile takes this concept a step further: the framework allows pages to be cached even before they're linked to or displayed in the browser. Taking advantage of this functionality is as easy as using an HTML attribute named data-prefetch. Simply add it to any hyperlink in your webpage, and once the webpage has loaded, the URLs that these hyperlinks point to will be preloaded and cached. The following line of code shows how to add this attribute to a hyperlink to preload and cache the page it's pointing to:

```
<a href="page2.html" data-prefetch>Link to page 2</a>
```

When running this example in a web browser, the request is made immediately upon page load. **Figure 4.2** shows an example of the XMLHttpRequest being made from Chrome when the page loads.

The framework also provides a way to handle page preloading via the application programming interface (API). We'll talk more specifically about the API later in the book, but it's important to know how to access it.

NOTE: The application programming interface (API) allows for communication among multiple pieces of software.

To preload pages programmatically, you first need to access the jQuery Mobile object:

```
$.mobile
```

Once the document object is ready, use the loadPage method to pass the URL you want to preload and define a number of properties for the request:

```
$(document).ready(function() {
    $.mobile.loadPage( "page2.html", {
        type: false,
        reloadPage: false,
        type: 'get'
    });
});
```

There are quite a few arguments you can pass as options in the loadPage method. **Table 4.4** lists those optional arguments.

TABLE 4.4 loadPage optional arguments

ARGUMENT	DESCRIPTION
data	Holds an object or string that can be sent with an Ajax page request.
loadMsgDelay	Sets the number of milliseconds to delay before showing the load message. The default is 50 milliseconds.
pageContainer	Holds the loaded page. The default is the jQuery Mobile page container, but this is customizable.
reloadPage	Defines whether or not to reload the page being requested. The default value is false.
role	When the page is loaded, this defines the data-role value that will be applied.
type	Specifies whether the request is a get or a post.

In addition to providing control for preloading files, the jQuery Mobile framework provides control for caching pages in the document object model (DOM). Just like the preload option, you can define whether a page should be cached in the DOM via an HTML attribute or the jQuery Mobile API. The following example shows how the attribute can be used in a page tag to cache a webpage:

```
<div data-role="page" data-dom-cache="true">
```

To cache a webpage using the API, you can set all pages to cache by default:

```
$.mobile.page.prototype.options.domCache = true;
```

Or, you can cache a page independently. You would cache a page with an id of my-page like so:

```
$('#my-page').page(true);
```

When working with the single-page template, jQuery Mobile also manages the pages it preloads so the DOM doesn't get too large. If many pages are kept in the DOM, the browser's memory usage can get out of control and the browser will likely slow down or crash. To manage the memory size, the framework removes pages that are loaded via Ajax from the DOM automatically via the pagehide event when the visitor navigates away from them. You'll learn more about this and other events later in the book.

There are a number of benefits to preloading and caching pages. They load quicker and prevent the Ajax loading message from appearing when a visitor tries to access the preloaded page. However, it's important to keep in mind that each preloaded page creates an additional HTTP request, which uses more bandwidth. Therefore, it's important to preload pages only when you think visitors are likely to view a subsequent webpage.

WORKING WITH PAGE TRANSITIONS

A number of page transitions can be used with the jQuery Mobile framework. All the page transitions are CSS-based effects. When using Ajax navigation, the page transitions work between linked pages or form submissions. **Table 4.5** lists the available page transitions in the framework.

TABLE 4.5 Page transitions

METHOD	DESCRIPTION
slide	Slides the hyperlinked page in from the right to replace the current page. Slide is the default page transition.
slideup	Slides the hyperlinked page up to replace the current page.
slidedown	Slides the hyperlinked page down from the top to replace the current page.
pop	Zooms the hyperlinked page in from the center of the current page and replaces it.
fade	Fades in the hyperlinked page over the current page and replaces it.
flip	Creates a 3D effect where the hyperlinked page appears to be on the backside of the current page as it flips and the hyperlinked page comes into view.

NOTE: Use the flip transition with caution, because it is supported only by browsers that support 3D CSS transform rendering.

Each of these page transitions is easy to set up globally as a default using the defaultPageTransition property. To set it up properly, it's necessary to bind to the mobileinit event, which is accessible through the API via the jQuery Mobile object:

```
$(document).bind("mobileinit", function() {
    $.mobile.defaultPageTransition = 'fade';
});
```

The binding of the event handler needs to be executed before the jQuery Mobile library loads. Therefore, in your HTML file, arrange your JavaScript files in a specific order:

```
<script src="http://ajax.googleapis.com/ajax/libs/jquery/1.7.1/
➝ jquery.min.js"></script>
<script src="assets/js/custom-jqm-transitions.js"></script>
```

```
<script src="http://code.jquery.com/mobile/1.0.1/
→  jquery.mobile-1.0.1.min.js"></script>
```

They can also be set on a per-link basis to override the default page transition. This option is useful for a number of situations, such as creating pop-up windows that use the pop transition:

```
<a href="popup.html" data-transition="pop">Pop-up</a>
```

Or, form submissions that use the flip transition:

```
<form action="" method="get" data-transition="flip">
    <input type="text" name="name">
    <input type="submit" value="Submit">
</form>
```

It's even possible to set the page transition to none to disable the page transition for a particular hyperlink or form submission:

```
<form action="" method="get" data-transition="none">
    <input type="text" name="name">
    <input type="submit" value="Submit">
</form>
```

jQuery also creates a reverse transition by automatically applying the same page transition when the back button is pressed.

The complete example code for the global and individual page transitions looks like the following:

```
<!DOCTYPE html>
<html>
<head>
    <meta http-equiv="Content-Type" content="text/html;
    →  charset=UTF-8">
    <meta name="viewport" content="width=device-width,
    →  initial-scale=1">
```

```
<title>Page Transitions - jQuery Mobile: Design and Develop
    </title>
<link rel="stylesheet" href="http://code.jquery.com/
    mobile/1.0.1/jquery.mobile-1.0.1.min.css" />
<script src="http://ajax.googleapis.com/ajax/libs/jquery/1.7.1/
    jquery.min.js"></script>
<script src="assets/js/custom-jqm-transitions.js"></script>
<script src="http://code.jquery.com/mobile/1.0.1/
    jquery.mobile-1.0.1.min.js"></script>
</head>
<body class="container">
    <div data-role="page">
        <div data-role="header"><h1>Page Name</h1></div>
        <div data-role="content">
            <p><a href="popup.html" data-transition="pop">Pop-up
                </a></p>
            <form action="" method="get" data-transition="flip">
                <input type="text" name="name">
                <input type="submit" value="Submit">
            </form>
        </div>
        <div data-role="footer">Copyright</div>
    </div>
</body>
</html>
```

Beginning with the head of the document, you can see that the jQuery library is loaded first, then the custom JavaScript where the mobileinit event from our previous example is bound and the default page transition is set. Last, but not least, the jQuery Mobile library is loaded. Within the page there's a hyperlink that has a pop transition applied and a form that has a flip transition applied.

CUSTOMIZING LOADING MESSAGES

When pages are loading, a default message appears if there's a delay or if the page is not yet preloaded. The jQuery Mobile framework allows you to customize this message and a page-error loading message.

You can customize the loading message through the `loadingMessage` property. Set `loadingMessage` to any custom string by binding to the `mobileinit` event, which jQuery Mobile fires as soon as the document loads.

```
$(document).bind("mobileinit", function() {
    $.mobile.loadingMessage = 'Please wait';
});
```

This code will display a loading message that says "Please wait." The default message used for page loading is "Loading." The property can also be set to `false` to display no message at all:

```
$(document).bind("mobileinit", function() {
    $.mobile.loadingMessage = false;
});
```

When there is an error loading a page, jQuery Mobile displays a message that can also be customized through the API. The default message for page-load errors is "Error Loading Page." You can set the `pageLoadErrorMessage` property to any custom string as the error message:

```
$(document).bind("mobileinit", function() {
    $.mobile.pageLoadErrorMessage = 'There was an error, please try
    → again.';
});
```

WRAPPING **UP**

Working with pages is easy with jQuery Mobile: all you really need to know is basic HTML and a few mobile-related attributes. With most of the heavy lifting being done by the framework, it's easy to focus on the results of the website you're building. Understanding the internal functionality behind how pages work in jQuery Mobile is what begins to set you up for writing custom functionality. Customizing specific functionality in the messaging and behind the scenes helps to personalize your website. The level of customization that jQuery Mobile provides can be very useful in making a website more user-friendly. Visual indicators, like custom loading messages and page transitions, set expectations for visitors and provide them with a frame of reference, so they know when certain things are happening. Preloading and caching improves usability by speeding up page loads and giving visitors what they want when they want it. jQuery Mobile provides fine-grained control to enhance mobile websites in a custom way.

5

DIALOG WINDOWS AND **BUTTONS**

No mobile website or application is complete without dialog windows, pop-ups, and buttons to provide feedback and options to users. The jQuery Mobile framework lets you create all of these with the addition of a simple data-rel attribute.

CREATING A BASIC DIALOG WINDOW

Creating a basic dialog window is easy with jQuery Mobile. Just use the data-rel attribute on any anchor tag and set its value to dialog:

data-rel="dialog"

Dialog windows can be included with a page or pages in a single HTML file just like a multipage template, or they can be external webpages like a single-page template. To create a multipage template that includes a dialog window, you simply add another jQuery Mobile page—the difference is in how you link to it. In other words, any page can be a dialog window; what makes it a dialog is the way it's opened. The following example shows a hyperlink with a data-rel attribute, which opens a page in a dialog window:

```
<!DOCTYPE html>
<html>
<head>
    <meta http-equiv="Content-Type" content="text/html;
    →  charset=UTF-8">
    <meta name="viewport" content="width=device-width,
    →  initial-scale=1">
    <title>Dialog - jQuery Mobile: Design and Develop</title>
    <link rel="stylesheet" href="http://code.jquery.com/
    →  mobile/1.0.1/jquery.mobile-1.0.1.min.css" />
    <script src="http://ajax.googleapis.com/ajax/libs/jquery/1.7.1/
    →  jquery.min.js"></script>
    <script src="http://code.jquery.com/mobile/1.0.1/
    →  jquery.mobile-1.0.1.min.js"></script>
</head>
<body>
    <div data-role="page">
        <div data-role="header"><h1>Dialog Test</h1></div>
        <div data-role="content">
            <p><a href="#multipage-dialog" data-rel=
            →  "dialog">Open Multi-page Dialog</a></p>
```

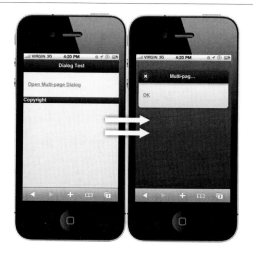

FIGURE 5.1 A multipage dialog window.

```
        </div>
    <div data-role="footer">Copyright</div>
  </div>
  <div data-role="page" id="multipage-dialog">
        <div data-role="header"><h1>Multi-page dialog window
        →  </h1></div>
        <div data-role="content">
            <p><a href="dialog.html" data-rel="back">OK</a></p>
        </div>
  </div>
</body>
</html>
```

In this example, there are two pages: the first page is displayed by default. Within this default page there's a hyperlink that has a data-rel="dialog" and a link to an anchor. The anchor that's being linked to is the ID of the second page. The second page is set up like any jQuery Mobile page: it's opened as a dialog because of the way it's linked to. **Figure 5.1** shows the result of this code.

As mentioned, dialog windows can also be external webpages that are linked to via a hyperlink with a data-rel="dialog" attribute and value. The following example is very similar to the previous one, with the main difference being that the hyperlink is now pointing to an external HTML file called dialog-window.html:

```
<!DOCTYPE html>
<html>
<head>
    <meta http-equiv="Content-Type" content="text/html;
    → charset=UTF-8">
    <meta name="viewport" content="width=device-width,
    → initial-scale=1">
    <title>Dialog - jQuery Mobile: Design and Develop</title>
    <link rel="stylesheet" href="http://code.jquery.com/
    → mobile/1.0.1/jquery.mobile-1.0.1.min.css" />
    <script src="http://ajax.googleapis.com/ajax/libs/jquery/1.7.1/
    → jquery.min.js"></script>
    <script src="http://code.jquery.com/mobile/1.0.1/
    → jquery.mobile-1.0.1.min.js"></script>
</head>
<body>
    <div data-role="page">
            <div data-role="header"><h1>Dialog Test</h1></div>
            <div data-role="content">
                <p><a href="dialog-window.html" data-rel="dialog">
                → Open External Dialog</a></p>
            </div>
        <div data-role="footer">Copyright</div>
    </div>
</body>
</html>
```

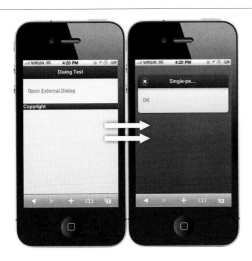

FIGURE 5.2 A single-page dialog window.

The HTML file that's being linked to can be set up like any jQuery Mobile webpage:

```
<!DOCTYPE html>
<html>
<head>
    <meta http-equiv="Content-Type" content="text/html; charset=UTF-8">
    <title>Dialog - jQuery Mobile: Design and Develop</title>
</head>
<body>
    <div data-role="page">
            <div data-role="header"><h1>Single-page dialog window
            → </h1></div>
        <div data-role="content">
            <p><a href="#" data-rel="back">OK</a></p>
        </div>
    </div>
</body>
</html>
```

The result of this code looks like **Figure 5.2**.

jQuery Mobile dialogs can also be used as pop-up windows. Rather than loading a dialog that typically provides or asks for feedback, the dialog can be another webpage that includes copy, media, and so on. In the following example, the dialog is used to open a YouTube video in a pop-up window:

```
<!DOCTYPE html>
<html>
<head>
    <meta http-equiv="Content-Type" content="text/html; charset=UTF-8">
    <meta name="viewport" content="width=device-width,
    → initial-scale=1">
    <title>Pop-up - jQuery Mobile: Design and Develop</title>
    <link rel="stylesheet" href="http://code.jquery.com/
    → mobile/1.0.1/jquery.mobile-1.0.1.min.css" />
    <script src="http://ajax.googleapis.com/ajax/libs/jquery/1.7.1/
    → jquery.min.js"></script>
    <script src="http://code.jquery.com/mobile/1.0.1/
    → jquery.mobile-1.0.1.min.js"></script>
    <style type="text/css">
        .ui-dialog .ui-header,
        .ui-dialog .ui-content,
        .ui-dialog .ui-footer {
            max-width: 640px;
        }
    </style>
</head>
<body>
    <div data-role="page">
        <div data-role="header"><h1>Pop-up Test</h1></div>
        <div data-role="content">
            <p>President Barack Obama's Inaugural Address</p>
            <p><a href="popup-window.html" data-rel="dialog">
            → Play now &gt;</a></p>
```

```
            </div>
            <div data-role="footer">Copyright</div>
        </div>
    </body>
</html>
```

Dialog windows have a predefined width, but these can be overwritten via the .ui-dialog classes. The HTML file in this example that's being loaded as a pop-up window includes a YouTube video of President Obama's inaugural address. Since the video is 640 x 360 pixels, the max-width has been set to 640. However, since the width of a mobile device can be much smaller than 640 pixels, the width for the video iFrame in the pop-up window has been set to 100%. This allows the video to fill the width of the pop-up window regardless of the size, with a max-width of 640 pixels:

```
<!DOCTYPE html>
<html>
<head>
    <meta http-equiv="Content-Type" content="text/html; charset=UTF-8">
    <title>Pop-up - jQuery Mobile: Design and Develop</title>
</head>
<body>
    <div data-role="page">
        <div data-role="header"><h1>President Barack Obama's
        ⟶  Inaugural Address</h1></div>
        <div data-role="content">
            <iframe width="100%" height="360" src="http://
            ⟶  www.youtube.com/embed/3PuHGKnboNY" frameborder="0"
            ⟶  allowfullscreen></iframe>
        </div>
    </div>
</body>
</html>
```

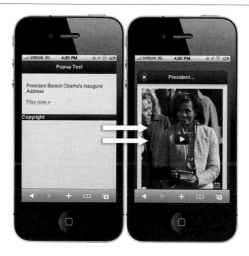

FIGURE 5.3 A custom pop-up window with video.

By default, the dialog (or pop-up) window includes a Close button, so you don't need to add any other hyperlinks or functionality to the dialog window. **Figure 5.3** shows an example of the video pop-up window with President Obama's inaugural address.

Dialog windows also include transitions. The default transition is pop, but this transition can be changed to flip or slidedown. To change the transition, add the data-transition attribute to the hyperlink that includes the data-rel="dialog" setting. If we were to add a slidedown data-transition to the previous example, the code would look like this:

```
<a href="popup-window.html" data-rel="dialog" data-transition=
  "slidedown">Play now &gt;</a>
```

WORKING WITH BUTTONS

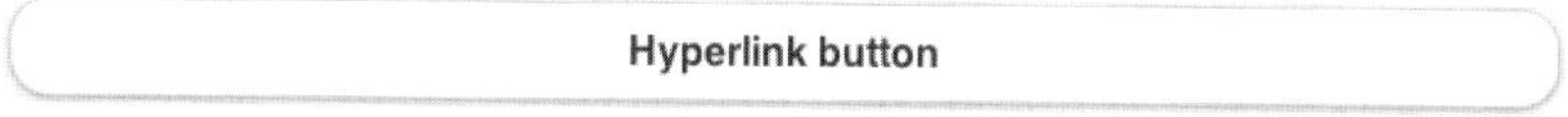

FIGURE 5.4 A hyperlink element that has a `data-role` of `button`.

FIGURE 5.5 A hyperlink element that has a `data-inline` set to `true`.

jQuery Mobile provides a way to create buttons with HTML anchor and input elements. Buttons offer a more usable alternative to standard hyperlinks and inputs by creating a larger clickable area. To convert a hyperlink into a button, set the `data-role` attribute to `button` (**Figure 5.4**):

```
<a href="#" data-role="button">Hyperlink button</a>
```

By default, buttons are the full width of the containing element, but you can set them to inline by using the `data-inline` attribute. This attribute, when set to `true`, creates a button whose width is determined by the text in the hyperlink (**Figure 5.5**):

```
<a href="#" data-role="button" data-inline="true">Hyperlink button
→  </a>
```

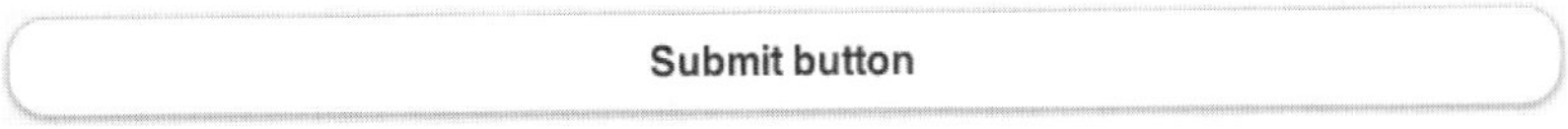

> **Submit button**

FIGURE 5.6 A Submit button that has a `data-role` equal to `button`.

Buttons can be enhanced by a number of additional `data-` attributes. **Table 5.1** lists all the possible button `data-` attributes and their values.

TABLE 5.1 Button `data-` attributes

data- ATTRIBUTES	VALUES
data-corners	true | false (true is the default value)
data-icon	home | delete | plus | arrow-u | arrow-d | check | gear | grid | star | custom | arrow-r | arrow-l | minus | refresh | forward | back | alert | info | search
data-iconpos	left | right | top | bottom | notext (left is the default value)
data-iconshadow	true | false (true is the default value)
data-inline	true | false (false is the default value)
data-shadow	true | false (true is the default value)
data-theme	swatch letter (a–z)

Input buttons differ from hyperlinks in that they all default to a button. The following Submit button defaults to a jQuery Mobile button:

```
<input type="submit" value="Submit button">
```

There's nothing special about this input element. **Figure 5.6** shows an example of what this input button looks like when enhanced with jQuery Mobile.

Many types of input elements are auto-enhanced by jQuery Mobile as buttons. These include input elements with a type attribute set to either `button`, `submit`, `reset`, or image, all of which look the same by default. The only way to change this default enhancement is to set the `data-role` to a value of `none`.

Buttons can include an icon using the `data-icon` attribute. The number of default icons is pretty impressive, and the icons are extremely easy to use. **Table 5.2** shows an example of each of the icons that you can add to jQuery Mobile buttons by using the `data-icon` attribute.

TABLE 5.2 Button icons

NAME	ATTRIBUTE	ICON
Left arrow	`data-icon="arrow-l"`	
Right arrow	`data-icon="arrow-r"`	
Up arrow	`data-icon="arrow-u"`	
Down arrow	`data-icon="arrow-d"`	
Delete	`data-icon="delete"`	
Plus	`data-icon="plus"`	
Minus	`data-icon="minus"`	
Check	`data-icon="check"`	
Gear	`data-icon="gear"`	
Refresh	`data-icon="refresh"`	
Forward	`data-icon="forward"`	
Back	`data-icon="back"`	
Grid	`data-icon="grid"`	
Star	`data-icon="star"`	
Alert	`data-icon="alert"`	
Info	`data-icon="info"`	
Home	`data-icon="home"`	
Search	`data-icon="search"`	

FIGURE 5.7 An example of a button using the `notext` `data-iconpos` with a home `data-icon`.

FIGURE 5.8 A custom checkmark icon.

Button icons can be positioned in a number of different locations. To do this, use the `data-iconpos` attribute and set it to one of the following values:

- `left` (left is the default)

- `right`

- `top`

- `bottom`

- `notext` (As seen in **Figure 5.7**, this value uses only the icon, hiding the text within the hyperlink or input value.)

Custom icons can also be used via CSS. To create a custom icon, you first need to choose a name value. For the purposes of this demo we'll use `checkmark`. Using this value in the `data-icon` attribute for a hyperlink or input that uses the button plug-in generates a CSS class. The CSS class includes ui-icon- before the custom value, so the CSS class for the custom value we defined is `ui-icon-checkmark`. With this class in place, you can easily target the class and add a background image as the icon:

```
.ui-icon-checkmark {
    background-image: url("5-custom-icon.png");
}
```

FIGURE 5.9 A custom checkmark icon when used as a button icon.

When designing the icon, you'll want to create an 18 x 18 pixel PNG-8 with alpha transparency to match the built-in jQuery Mobile icons. **Figure 5.8** shows an example of the custom icon.

Now that we have created this icon and a CSS class associated with it, we can assign the icon to a button. To assign our new icon to a button, we simply use the data-icon attribute and set it to checkmark:

```
<a href="#checkmark" data-role="button" data-icon="checkmark">
→ Checkmark example</a>
```

The final result of this code looks similar to **Figure 5.9**.

WRAPPING **UP**

The items in this chapter are the foundation of any mobile website or application. Having the ability to provide feedback or ask for feedback from a user through a dialog window is essential. Launching content in modal windows is the norm these days, eliminating annoying pop-up windows. And buttons provide a way to enhance any hyperlink or input button into a clickable, user-friendly solution.

6

WORKING WITH **TOOLBARS**

The jQuery Mobile framework offers toolbar widgets that let you easily define headers and footers. As with other widgets, toolbars are defined by data- attributes with normal HTML markup and enhanced by the framework when the webpage renders. Toolbars can contain navigation buttons and be set in fixed positions at the top or bottom of your mobile webpages. This chapter covers all the toolbar possibilities and offers examples of each.

jQuery Mobile offers two types of toolbars: headers and footers. This section covers both.

HEADER TOOLBARS

Header toolbars are the perfect way to provide a page title, navigation, or other common calls to action, such as Save or Cancel buttons, in a web application. Header toolbars are typically the first element in a mobile webpage. If a page title is used in a header toolbar, any of the HTML heading-level elements can be used to contain the title. Without a heading element, page titles contain no margin and are not center-aligned as they are with heading elements; rather, they look like the toolbar in **Figure 6.1**.

A heading element yields a result that looks much nicer than Figure 6.1. Heading elements also allow for semantic webpages and flexibility in how elements are used. The header element code we've been using thus far looks like the following example:

```
<div data-role="header">
    <h1>My Page Title</h1>
</div>
```

As you can see, the header is defined by a simple data-role attribute that has a value of header. In this example, an h1 element has been added to define the page title. Using this h1 element produces the results shown in **Figure 6.2**.

FIGURE 6.1 A header toolbar without a page title.

FIGURE 6.2 A header toolbar with a page title.

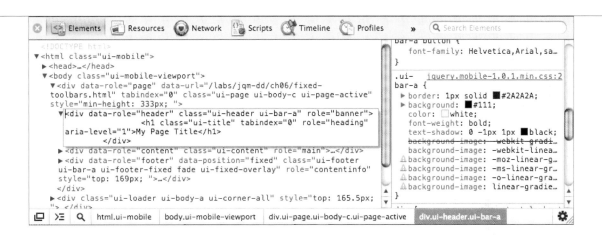

When jQuery Mobile enhances the HTML, the header toolbar code looks dramatically different. As shown in **Figure 6.3**, viewing the HTML markup with Chrome's Developer Tools reveals the many extra attributes added after the framework has made its enhancements.

FIGURE 6.3 Header markup after jQuery Mobile enhancements.

The Cascading Style Sheet (CSS) classes are added to the div element, which sets the positioning to relative, adds a border, sets the font color, and more. Here's a closer look at the enhancements that the framework makes to the actual HTML markup:

```
<div data-role="header" class="ui-header ui-bar-a" role="banner">

    <h1 class="ui-title" tabindex="0" role="heading"
 →  aria-level="1">My Page Title</h1>

</div>
```

Another noticeable difference is that the heading element includes a ui-title class. This class sets a combination of properties that center the text, add a margin, create ellipses for overflowing text, and more. The framework also adds a tabindex that automatically makes the webpages more accessible by creating a logical tabbing sequence, which is used by mobile devices like iOS with their built-in Next button. Headers can also include elements other than headings; buttons, for example, can be important additions to your toolbars.

ADDING BUTTONS

With the button options discussed in Chapter 5, "Dialog Windows and Buttons," and an unlimited number of custom icons, you can address any functional requirements you can imagine. Headers are a great location to prominently display important buttons in a mobile web application, and it's easy to do so using jQuery Mobile. The following example shows how to add a Save button to a header element in a dialog window to edit a user profile:

```
<!DOCTYPE html>

<html>

<head>

    <meta http-equiv="Content-Type" content="text/html;
    → charset=UTF-8">

    <meta name="viewport" content="width=device-width,
    → initial-scale=1">

    <title>Header Toolbar - jQuery Mobile: Design and Develop
    → </title>

    <link rel="stylesheet" href="http://code.jquery.com/
    → mobile/1.0.1/jquery.mobile-1.0.1.min.css" />

    <script src="http://ajax.googleapis.com/ajax/libs/jquery/1.7.1/
    → jquery.min.js"></script>

    <script src="http://code.jquery.com/mobile/1.0.1/
    → jquery.mobile-1.0.1.min.js"></script>

</head>

<body>

    <div data-role="page">

        <div data-role="header">

            <h1>John Doe</h1>

            <a href="#options-dialog" data-icon="gear" class=
            → "ui-btn-right" data-rel="dialog">Edit Profile</a>

        </div>

        <div data-role="content">
```

```html
            <p>123 E Street</p>
            <p>Chicago, Il 60622</p>
        </div>
    </div>
    <div data-role="page" id="options-dialog">
        <div data-role="header">
            <h1>Edit John Doe</h1>
            <a href="#" data-icon="check">Save</a>
        </div>
        <div data-role="content">
            <label for="profile-image">Profile Image</label>
            <p><img src="assets/img/profile.png"></p>
            <input type="file" id="profile-image"
            ⇢ name="profile-image">
            <label for="street-address">Street Address</label>
            <input type="text" id="street-address"
            ⇢ name="street-address" value="123 E Street">
            <label for="city">City</label>
            <input type="text" id="city" name="city"
            ⇢ value="Chicago">
            <label for="state">State</label>
            <input type="text" id="state" name="state" value="Il">
            <label for="zip-code">Zip Code</label>
            <input type="text" id="zip-code" name="zip-code"
            ⇢ value="60622">
        </div>
    </div>
</body>
</html>
```

FIGURE 6.4 A header toolbar with a Save button.

FIGURE 6.5 Grouped buttons.

Using the single-page template, a second page is added and a hyperlink is set to open it as a dialog window from the default page. In the dialog window, the Save button is visually represented by the appropriate `data-icon` attribute value. The Option button in the default page uses a gear, and the Save button uses a check-mark. **Figure 6.4** illustrates a way to display an editable form in a dialog window to modify a user profile. After updating the input values, the user can click the Save button. You could put code in place to process the user's updates and store them in a database.

Buttons can also be grouped, rather than displayed individually. To group buttons, simply add a `div` as a container around them and apply a `data-role` with a value of `controlgroup` with a `data-type` set to `horizontal`:

```
<div data-role="header">

    <div data-role="controlgroup" data-type="horizontal">

        <a href="#" data-role="button" data-icon="delete">Delete</a>

        <a href="#" data-role="button" data-icon="check">Save</a>

    </div>

</div>
```

You'll also notice that there are `data-role` attributes set as `button`. This attribute and value must be added to buttons within a `controlgroup`, otherwise the hyperlinks won't render as buttons. **Figure 6.5** shows that this example renders a toolbar with a combined Delete and Save button, so the two no longer appear separate.

Multiple groups can also be added to a toolbar to visually separate the groups from one another:

```
<div data-role="header">
    <div data-role="controlgroup" data-type="horizontal"
    ↪ class="align-left">
        <a href="#" data-role="button" data-icon="home">Home</a>
            <a href="#" data-role="button"
            ↪ data-icon="arrow-l">Back</a>
    </div>
        <div data-role="controlgroup" data-type="horizontal"
        ↪ class="align-right">
            <a href="#" data-role="button"
            ↪ data-icon="delete">Delete</a>
            <a href="#" data-role="button" data-icon="check">Save</a>
        </div>
</div>
```

FIGURE 6.6 Multiple sets of grouped buttons.

These groups of buttons are also using custom classes that align one set left and the other right. The CSS for these classes is a simple float left and a float right:

```
<style type="text/css">
.align-left {
    float: left;
}
.align-right {
    float: right;
}
</style>
```

Figure 6.6 shows these two groups of buttons and how they are separated in a header toolbar.

FOOTER TOOLBARS

Footer toolbars are like header toolbars except that they typically reside at the bottom, rather than the top, of a webpage. They are often used to display copyright notices and other similar information.

```
<div data-role="footer">
    <h4>Copyright</h4>
</div>
```

As with page titles in header toolbars, any text that's added to the footer toolbar needs a heading element to include spacing, alignment, and so on. The following code example shows the markup for footer toolbars after it's enhanced by the framework:

```
<div data-role="footer" class="ui-footer ui-bar-a"
→ role="contentinfo">
    <h4 class="ui-title" tabindex="0" role="heading"
    → aria-level="1">Copyright</h4>
</div>
```

Although footer toolbars are a good place for copyrights and the like, it's also possible to include all the same markup as a header toolbar, including buttons, navbars, and so on.

POSITIONING TOOLBARS

You can position toolbars as fixed or fullscreen. Fixed toolbars are always visible on the webpage. When a header toolbar is fixed, it always appears at the top, even when the page is scrolled. When a footer toolbar is fixed, it is always visible at the very bottom of the web browser. To add fixed positioning to toolbars, all that's needed is a data-position attribute with a value of fixed:

```
<div data-role="page">
    <div data-role="header" data-position="fixed">
        <h1>Page Title</h1>
    </div>
    <div data-role="content">
        <p>Body Copy</p>
    </div>
    <div data-role="footer" data-position="fixed">
        <h4>Copyright</h4>
    </div>
</div>
```

FIGURE 6.7 Fixed toolbars.

Figure 6.7 shows how these toolbars render in a web browser.

The result of this code functions like fixed positioning works with CSS, but jQuery Mobile doesn't use CSS for this functionality. Since fixed positioning is not supported by many mobile browsers, jQuery Mobile uses dynamic repositioning instead.

You can also update the position of toolbars via the jQuery Mobile API. Using this method is sometimes necessary, for example, when a widget, such as an accordion, is expanded and the page changes height. You can call the following code to update the toolbar position:

```
$.mobile.fixedToolbars.show(true);
```

This code is great to use when you're building dynamic content.

In addition to fixed toolbars, you can create fullscreen fixed headers. Fullscreen fixed headers are the same as fixed ones, the only difference being that the content sits behind the toolbars, so the content is still fullscreen and the toolbars are transparent. The toolbars also disappear when the page is clicked. To create fullscreen fixed toolbars, just add the data-fullscreen attribute and set it to true:

```
<div data-role="header" data-fullscreen="true"
→ data-position="fixed">
    <h1>Page Title</h1>
</div>
```

With regular fixed toolbars, the content sits between the header and the footer. Fullscreen toolbars are common for video players or photo slideshows.

CREATING **NAVIGATION BARS**

Navigation is most prominently displayed in the header of a webpage. jQuery Mobile offers a widget to create navigation called navbar. Navbars are not required to be in a header toolbar, but they're typically seen in either a header or footer. Let's look at how one can be used effectively as page navigation in the header of a mobile website. A navbar is essentially a simple unordered list contained within an element that includes a data-role value of navbar:

```
<div data-role="header">

    <div data-role="navbar">

        <ul>

            <li><a href="/">Home</a></li>

            <li><a href="#">About</a></li>

            <li><a href="#">Contact</a></li>

        </ul>

    </div>

</div>
```

Once again jQuery Mobile makes it incredibly easy to transform simple HTML markup into a visually appealing and functional widget by adding a single attribute. **Figure 6.8** shows how this code renders visually.

The cool thing about the framework is that it evenly divides the space of the navbar based on the number of buttons. This is why each of the buttons in Figure 6.8 is proportionate. The only caveat about navbars is that if they contain more than five hyperlinks they'll begin wrapping to multiple lines, as seen in **Figure 6.9**.

Although this is a limitation in one sense, it's also a saving grace because mobile devices simply don't have the room to accommodate this many buttons in a horizontal space.

FIGURE 6.8 A navbar used in a header toolbar.

FIGURE 6.9 A navbar with more than five buttons.

FIGURE 6.10 A navbar and a logo in a header.

Another nice thing about navbars in headers is that they don't require you to eliminate the page title. You can still use a heading element with a page title and then add a navbar underneath. Or, better yet, you can add a logo and then a navbar, like you typically see across the web:

```
<div data-role="header">
    <img src="assets/img/trademark-jquerymobiletv.png">
    <div data-role="navbar">
        <ul>
            <li><a href="/">Home</a></li>
            <li><a href="#">About</a></li>
            <li><a href="#">Contact</a></li>
        </ul>
    </div>
</div>
```

As shown in **Figure 6.10**, the logo is added above the navigation. Header toolbars can include a number of elements; they're not limited to buttons or page titles.

Figure 6.11 shows an example of a navbar that includes button icons.

This example shows what's possible with the framework when you combine widgets to create functionality.

FIGURE 6.11 A navbar with button icons and a logo in a header.

WRAPPING **UP**

Toolbars can help you create consistency in a mobile website by adding page titles that have the same look and feel, navigation bars, or a combination of branding and functional elements. In addition to look and feel, understanding how to leverage headers and footers to create a more usable website is important and toolbars offer the functionality needed to achieve this.

7
LAYOUT OPTIONS

jQuery Mobile is flexible in the sense that it's based on standard HTML and CSS, so the layout options are essentially endless. However, the framework does offer a few enhancements in the form of widgets you can use to organize content and create custom layouts without writing additional code. Using data- attributes and standard CSS classes, the framework transforms the markup used to structure these widgets. In this chapter, you'll learn how to create grids, collapsible content, and accordions.

GRIDS

Although jQuery Mobile still supports standard HTML tables, the framework also offers a simple alternative in the form of a widget called grids. Grids let you position elements next to one another. They're useful for smaller elements such as buttons and icons, but not recommended for large items or chunks of copy, since mobile device resolution is much lower than the desktop environment and usability is extremely diminished.

GRID COLUMNS

With jQuery Mobile, you can create up to a five-column grid using the four pre-defined grid-column layout options shown in **Table 7.1**. Each column is based on an individual CSS class with a naming convention that starts with the prefix ui-grid.

TABLE 7.1 Columns and CSS classes

COLUMNS	CSS CLASS
Two-column	ui-grid-a
Three-column	ui-grid-b
Four-column	ui-grid-c
Five-column	ui-grid-d

Creating a grid is easy once you determine how many columns you want: just add the corresponding CSS class. The class for a two-column grid is ui-grid-a. This will be added to a container element, in this case two div elements that act as the two columns. Grid columns are defined HTML elements that include the ui-block class prefix; the prefix is appended with a letter in alphabetical order based on its position. For example, the first column's CSS class is ui-block-a, the second column's class is ui-block-b, and so on:

```
<div class="ui-grid-a">
    <div class="ui-block-a"><strong>2-Column</strong></div>
    <div class="ui-block-b">Column</div>
</div>
```

The layout that is rendered based on this code will look similar to **Figure** 7.1.

Within the columns, it's possible to add HTML, but as mentioned earlier, it's important to keep grid data to a minimum to accommodate the minimal width of mobile devices. Creating additional columns is as easy as using the corresponding ui-grid class and adding column blocks. The following example includes all the column types in a single HTML file with hr elements:

```
<div class="ui-grid-a">
    <div class="ui-block-a"><strong>2-Column</strong></div>
    <div class="ui-block-b">Column</div>
</div>
<hr>
<div class="ui-grid-b">
    <div class="ui-block-a"><strong>3-Column</strong></div>
    <div class="ui-block-b">Column</div>
    <div class="ui-block-c">Column</div>
</div>
<hr>
<div class="ui-grid-c">
    <div class="ui-block-a"><strong>4-Column</strong></div>
    <div class="ui-block-b">Column</div>
    <div class="ui-block-c">Column</div>
    <div class="ui-block-d">Column</div>
</div>
<hr>
```

FIGURE 7.1 A two-column grid.

```
<div class="ui-grid-d">

    <div class="ui-block-a"><strong>5-Column</strong></div>

    <div class="ui-block-b">Column</div>

    <div class="ui-block-c">Column</div>

    <div class="ui-block-d">Column</div>

    <div class="ui-block-e">Column</div>

</div>
```

The result of this code will look similar to **Figure 7.2**.

On their own, columns are pretty bland, but you can add predefined jQuery Mobile classes or write your own CSS for the existing classes. For example, the jQuery Mobile framework includes a class called `ui-bar` that adds padding and another set of classes that can be appended with a letter to customize the theme, which will affect the background, miscellaneous font styling, and so on. We'll learn more about jQuery Mobile themes later in the book. The following example uses the `ui-bar-a` class to add a blue background gradient, font styling, and other CSS updates:

FIGURE 7.2 Multiple grids with different column amounts.

```
<div class="ui-grid-a">

    <div class="ui-block-a">

        <div class="ui-bar ui-bar-b"><strong>2-Column</strong></div>

    </div>

    <div class="ui-block-b">

        <div class="ui-bar ui-bar-b">Column</div>

    </div>

</div>
```

Figure 7.3 shows the result of this code, which looks much nicer than the previous examples, adding styling updates that enhance the grid.

Adding custom CSS to a grid column is simple. Since the grid is standard HTML markup, you can append a custom CSS class to any of the elements. In the following example, a custom class block-title has been added to the first column and another class has been added to all div elements in the grid:

```
<!DOCTYPE html>

<html>

<head>

    <meta http-equiv="Content-Type" content="text/html;
    → charset=UTF-8">

    <meta name="viewport" content="width=device-width,
    → initial-scale=1">

    <title>Grids - jQuery Mobile: Design and Develop</title>

    <link rel="stylesheet" href="http://code.jquery.com/
    → mobile/1.0.1/jquery.mobile-1.0.1.min.css" />

    <script src="http://ajax.googleapis.com/ajax/libs/jquery/1.7.1/
    → jquery.min.js"></script>

    <script src="http://code.jquery.com/mobile/1.0.1/
    → jquery.mobile-1.0.1.min.js"></script>

    <style type="text/css">

    .ui-grid-a div {

        background-color: #ccc;

    }

    .ui-grid-a div.block-title {

        background-color: #fff;

    }

    </style>

</head>
```

FIGURE 7.3 A two-column grid with the ui-bar class.

FIGURE 7.4 A two-column grid with custom CSS applied.

```
<body>
    <div data-role="page">
        <div data-role="header" data-position="fixed">
            <h1>My Page Title</h1>
        </div>
        <div data-role="content">
            <div class="ui-grid-a">
                <div class="ui-block-a block-title">2-Column</div>
                <div class="ui-block-b">Column</div>
            </div>
        </div>
        <div data-role="footer" data-position="fixed">
            <h4>Copyright</h4>
        </div>
    </div>
</body>
</html>
```

The result of this code will look similar to **Figure 7.4**.

Using a two-column grid would have been a better way to handle the functionality for the button groups discussed in Chapter 5, "Dialog Windows and Buttons." Rather than using floats to align the control groups, you could use the grid to separate them. The following code shows how a grid could be used to create layouts within a toolbar:

```
<!DOCTYPE html>

<html>

<head>

    <meta http-equiv="Content-Type" content="text/html;
    →  charset=UTF-8">

    <meta name="viewport" content="width=device-width,
    →  initial-scale=1">

    <title>Grid with controlgroup - jQuery Mobile: Design and
    →  Develop</title>

    <link rel="stylesheet" href="http://code.jquery.com/
    →  mobile/1.0.1/jquery.mobile-1.0.1.min.css" />

    <script src="http://ajax.googleapis.com/ajax/libs/jquery/1.7.1/
    →  jquery.min.js"></script>

    <script src="http://code.jquery.com/mobile/1.0.1/
    →  jquery.mobile-1.0.1.min.js"></script>

    <style type="text/css">

        .ui-grid-a .ui-block-b {

            text-align: right;

        }

    </style>

</head>
```

```
<body>
    <div data-role="page">
        <div data-role="header">
            <div class="ui-grid-a">
                <div class="ui-block-a">
                    <div data-role="controlgroup"
                     →  data-type="horizontal">
                        <a href="#" data-role="button"
                         →  data-icon="home">Home</a>
                        <a href="#" data-role="button"
                         →  data-icon="arrow-l">Back</a>
                    </div>
                </div>
                <div class="ui-block-b">
                    <div data-role="controlgroup"
                     →  data-type="horizontal">
                        <a href="#" data-role="button"
                         →  data-icon="delete">Delete</a>
                        <a href="#" data-role="button"
                         →  data-icon="check">Save</a>
                    </div>
                </div>
            </div>
        </div>
        <div data-role="content">
            <p>Body Copy</p>
        </div>
        <div data-role="footer" data-position="fixed">
            <h4>Copyright</h4>
```

```
        </div>
      </div>
  </body>
</html>
```

Figure 7.5 shows the visual result of this code.

GRID ROWS

jQuery Mobile also lets you create grids with multiple rows. The same rules apply as with the classes used for columns; however, rows are defined by each new set of blocks that you add to a grid. For example, to create a four-column grid, the ui-grid-c class must be used as usual. Inside the grid is where things get different: simply repeat sets of block columns. In this case, it'll be multiple block sets in a four-column layout. The following example shows a four-column grid with two rows:

FIGURE 7.5 A grid being used to separate button control groups.

```
<div class="ui-grid-c">
    <div class="ui-block-a">
        <div class="ui-bar ui-bar-b">A</div>
    </div>
    <div class="ui-block-b">
        <div class="ui-bar ui-bar-b">B</div>
    </div>
    <div class="ui-block-c">
        <div class="ui-bar ui-bar-b">C</div>
    </div>
    <div class="ui-block-d">
        <div class="ui-bar ui-bar-b">D</div>
    </div>
```

FIGURE 7.6 A grid with multiple rows and columns.

```
<div class="ui-block-a">
    <div class="ui-bar ui-bar-b">A</div>
</div>
<div class="ui-block-b">
    <div class="ui-bar ui-bar-b">B</div>
</div>
<div class="ui-block-c">
    <div class="ui-bar ui-bar-b">C</div>
</div>
<div class="ui-block-d">
    <div class="ui-bar ui-bar-b">D</div>
</div>
</div>
```

Each element with the `ui-block-a` class automatically clears the row before it, resulting in a new row. When looking at the actual CSS included in the jQuery Mobile framework for the `ui-block-a` class, you can see that it clears left floats, therefore the result looks similar to **Figure 7.6**.

COLLAPSIBLE CONTENT

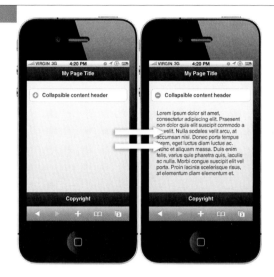

jQuery Mobile provides a widget that allows developers to create content that can expand and contract. This widget, referred to as collapsible content, includes a header and content area; the header acts as a button that can be touched to expand and contract the content area. To create a collapsible content area, apply the data-role attribute with a value of collapsible to a div that will be used to contain a heading and content area. In the following example, the container element with a data-role set to collapsible includes a heading and a paragraph element:

```
<div data-role="collapsible">

    <h3>Collapsible content header</h3>

    <p>Lorem ipsum dolor sit amet, consectetur adipiscing elit.
    → Praesent non dolor quis elit suscipit commodo a eu velit.
    → Nulla sodales velit arcu, at accumsan nisi. Donec porta
    → tempus lorem, eget luctus diam luctus ac. Nunc et aliquam
    → massa. Duis enim felis, varius quis pharetra quis, iaculis
    → ac nulla. Morbi congue suscipit elit vel porta. Proin lacinia
    → scelerisque risus, at elementum diam elementum et.</p>

</div>
```

By adding the collapsible data-role to the container, the heading element is automatically converted into a button that can be used to expand and contract the paragraph. Visually, the example will produce the sequence seen in **Figure 7.7**.

Collapsible content is a great way to organize large amounts of information. Showing lots of data all at one time can be overwhelming and deter people from accessing your valuable content. By hiding the content when the user first loads a webpage, content can remain organized and users can reveal only the content areas that they're interested in.

Collapsible content areas can also include a data- attribute called data-collapsed. By default, collapsible content areas are collapsed when the webpage is first loaded. The data-collapsed attribute provides a way to expand collapsible content areas when the page first loads. The following example shows the markup to accomplish this:

```
<div data-role="collapsible" data-collapsed="false">
    <h3>Collapsible content header</h3>
    <p>Lorem ipsum dolor sit amet, consectetur adipiscing elit.
     Praesent non dolor quis elit suscipit commodo a eu velit.
     Nulla sodales velit arcu, at accumsan nisi. Donec porta
     tempus lorem, eget luctus diam luctus ac. Nunc et aliquam
     massa. Duis enim felis, varius quis pharetra quis, iaculis
     ac nulla. Morbi congue suscipit elit vel porta. Proin lacinia
     scelerisque risus, at elementum diam elementum et.</p>
</div>
```

It's also possible to nest collapsible content by adding a collapsible content area inside another collapsible content area. The following example shows how to write the markup to create a nested collapsible content area:

```
<div data-role="collapsible" data-collapsed="false">
    <h3>Collapsible content header</h3>
    <p>Lorem ipsum dolor sit amet, consectetur adipiscing elit.</p>
    <div data-role="collapsible">
        <h3>Collapsible child #1</h3>
        <p>Lorem ipsum dolor sit amet.</p>
    </div>
```

FIGURE 7.8 The sequence of events that occurs when opening a nested collapsible content area.

```
<div data-role="collapsible">
    <h3>Collapsible child #2</h3>
    <p>Lorem ipsum dolor sit amet.</p>
</div>
</div>
```

The two highlighted collapsible content areas in this example are nested in the main collapsible area. The result of this nested collapsible content will look similar to **Figure 7.8**.

It's also possible to nest deeper; in fact, you can nest as deep as you'd like.

CREATING ACCORDIONS

Collapsible content areas can also be grouped to create an accordion. An accordion is essentially a group of collapsible content areas that are aware of one another. For example, when one collapsible content area is expanded, any expanded ones will close, so only one content area is expanded at a time.

To define an accordion, a container element must be created to contain a group of collapsible content areas. On this container element, a data-role must be set

FIGURE 7.9 An example of an accordion and how it functions.

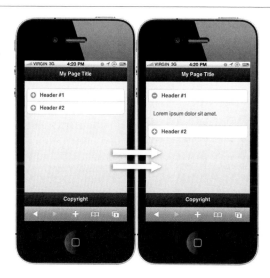

to the value `collapsible-set`. That's it. The following code shows the markup for an accordion with two collapsible content areas:

```
<div data-role="collapsible-set">
    <div data-role="collapsible">
        <h3>Header #1</h3>
        <p>Lorem ipsum dolor sit amet.</p>
    </div>
    <div data-role="collapsible">
        <h3>Header #2</h3>
        <p>Lorem ipsum dolor sit amet.</p>
    </div>
</div>
```

The code in this example creates an accordion that functions like the sequence shown in **Figure 7.9**.

WRAPPING **UP**

jQuery Mobile makes widgets incredibly easy to use, offering functionality that would otherwise require custom JavaScript or jQuery. Using a simple data- attribute or CSS class, the framework enhances these layout widgets and creates the required functionality. Handling layout differences between devices is another benefit of this framework: typically, CSS or JavaScript would need to be written to accommodate the varying dimensions of different devices. With jQuery Mobile you can use any custom HTML to create layouts, but it's always beneficial to determine whether the framework already includes a widget that can save you time.

8

WORKING
WITH LISTS

Lists are frequently used to display data in jQuery Mobile. The framework offers a plethora of formatting options to achieve just about any design pattern you can imagine, such as basic linked lists, numbered lists, nested lists, inset lists, split button lists, and lists with dividers, as well as lists with count bubbles, thumbnails, and icons. This chapter covers all these design patterns, providing example code and figures to show you how the end results should render.

BASIC LINKED LISTS

FIGURE 8.1 A basic linked list.

One of the most common design patterns you'll see with jQuery Mobile lists is a basic linked list. Often used to display navigation, basic linked lists are simply unordered lists that contain items with hyperlinks. jQuery Mobile enhances these lists when a `data-role` with a value of `listview` is attached to the opening tag of the unordered list element. The following markup shows how to create a basic linked list using the `listview` data-role:

```
<ul data-role="listview">
    <li><a href="#">Home</a></li>
    <li><a href="#">Articles</a></li>
    <li><a href="#">Videos</a></li>
    <li><a href="#">Books</a></li>
    <li><a href="#">More</a></li>
</ul>
```

This `listview` markup is enhanced by the framework to produce a list of links that includes arrow icons, background shadows, and more. **Figure 8.1** shows an example of the visual result of this markup.

Enhancements alter the markup, producing much different HTML. The next example shows a snippet of the markup after it's been enhanced by the framework. The opening unordered list tag and the first list item are shown to provide a sample of the enhancements, while the new portions are highlighted to show how much of the code has been enhanced. Note that the missing list items (`<!-- etc. -->`) are all altered in the same way as the first list item:

```
<ul data-role="listview" class="ui-listview">
    <li data-theme="c" class="ui-btn ui-btn-icon-right
     ⤳ ui-li-has-arrow ui-li ui-btn-up-c">
        <div class="ui-btn-inner ui-li" aria-hidden="true">
            <div class="ui-btn-text">
                <a href="#" class="ui-link-inherit">Home</a>
            </div>
            <span class="ui-icon ui-icon-arrow-r ui-icon-shadow">
             ⤳ </span>
        </div>
    </li>
<!-- etc. -->
```

As you can see, the framework makes a lot of additions to the code to produce the visual enhancements. First, a `ui-listview` class is added to set the margin, passing a `list-style`. Then the list items are updated with a `data-theme` attribute set to the c theme, and a group of CSS classes is added. We'll learn more about jQuery Mobile themes later in the book. The classes that are added are `ui-btn`, `ui-btn-icon-right`, `ui-li-has-arrow`, `ui-li`, and `ui-btn-up-c`. The names of the classes basically explain it all; for example, the `ui-btn` adds a pointer cursor,

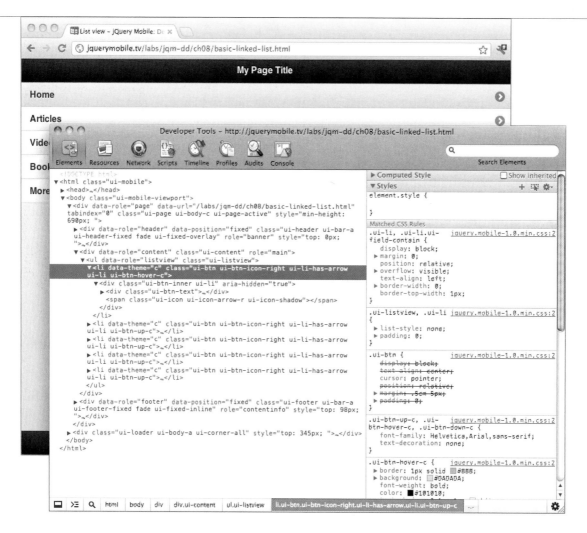

FIGURE 8.2 The custom CSS created by the framework.

sets the display to block, and adds some spacing to make it more touchable, while the `ui-btn-icon-right` tells the span element to align right with the arrow icon. Each of these CSS classes can be seen in-depth through a code inspector like the one in Chrome's Developer Tools. **Figure 8.2** shows some of the classes and their properties for a list item.

NUMBERED LISTS

You can create a numbered list from the same code using the `listview` data-role: simply convert the `ul` to an `ol`. The following example shows the modified code with numbered list items:

```
<ol data-role="listview">
    <li><a href="#">Home</a></li>
    <li><a href="#">Articles</a></li>
    <li><a href="#">Videos</a></li>
    <li><a href="#">Books</a></li>
    <li><a href="#">More</a></li>
</ol>
```

The visual result looks similar to **Figure 8.3**, with the numbers inset as part of the list item.

FIGURE 8.3 A basic numbered list.

NESTED LISTS

Nested lists are hidden by default and load like additional pages. When a list is nested within another list item, the parent list item becomes a hyperlink to the child list and a new `ui-page` is generated for that list via the framework. To create a nested list, simply take any list item and add another unordered or ordered list to it. In the following example, the `More` list item from our previous examples is configured as an `h2` heading with a description and a nested unordered list:

```
<ul data-role="listview">
    <li><a href="#">Home</a></li>
    <li><a href="#">Articles</a></li>
    <li><a href="#">Videos</a></li>
    <li><a href="#">Books</a></li>
    <li>
        <h2>More</h2>
        <p>Find more resources on jQuery Mobile</p>
```

FIGURE 8.4 A nested list appears after the More list item is selected.

```
<ul data-role="listview">

    <li><a href="http://www.jquerymobile.com">
    → jQuery Mobile</a></li>

    <li><a href="http://www.jquery.com">jQuery</a></li>

</ul>

</li>

</ul>
```

When the framework enhances the `listview`, the More list item becomes a hyperlink to the nested list, as seen in **Figure 8.4**.

The page generated from this nested list includes a header with the value of the list item title and then the nested list itself. Lists can be nested as deeply as you like; the framework will simply generate more and more pages.

INSET LISTS

By default, lists are set to the width of the device they are being viewed on; in other words, their width is always set to 100 percent. You can add an attribute to create what's known as an inset list, which looks like it's inset within the page (rather than extending to the edges of the device) and has rounded corners. The following example shows a basic linked list with the data-inset attribute set to true:

```
<ul data-role="listview" data-inset="true">
    <li><a href="#">Home</a></li>
    <li><a href="#">Articles</a></li>
    <li><a href="#">Videos</a></li>
    <li><a href="#">Books</a></li>
    <li><a href="#">More</a></li>
</ul>
```

Setting this attribute to true creates the visual results shown in **Figure 8.5**.

FIGURE 8.5 A basic linked list with the data-inset attribute set to true.

CUSTOMIZING LISTS

Once you understand how to create basic lists, you may find yourself wanting more options. Lists can be customized with dividers, thumbnails, icons, and more using data- attributes. This section shows you what attributes can be used and how to write the code for each of them.

SPLIT BUTTON LISTS

One option for providing additional list functionality is what's called a split button list. A split button list lets you provide two clickable options within the same list item. This is useful for items that require a link for details about a particular item as well as another action, such as a button to purchase the item or share it on a social network. Creating a split button list is easy: just add two anchor tags within a list item that uses the listview data-role:

```
<ul data-role="listview" data-split-icon="gear">
    <li>
        <a href="#item-detail">
            <h3>Using UI components in jQuery Mobile</h3>
            <p>Many UI components are available in the jQuery Mobile
            → framework.</p>
        </a>
        <a href="#item-purchase" data-rel="dialog">Buy now</a>
    </li>
    <li>
        <a href="#item-detail">
            <h3>Using the jQuery Mobile API</h3>
            <p>The jQuery Mobile API provides an extra level of
            → control over the customization of your mobile
            → website.</p>
        </a>
        <a href="#item-purchase" data-rel="dialog">Buy now</a>
    </li>
</ul>
```

FIGURE 8.6 A split button list with gear icons.

FIGURE 8.7 Icons available to the split-button-icon attribute.

The split button list in this example contains articles as list items that include a title and an overview. When selected, additional details can be viewed for a particular article. Each list item also includes a gear icon hyperlink that the user can click to pay for access to the article within a dialog window. The visual representation of this list is shown in **Figure 8.6**.

You can change the default icon for the split button that appears on the right side of the list item by using the `data-split-icon` attribute. The icons available with the `data-split-icon` attribute are the same as those available for buttons, as seen in **Figure 8.7**, but you can also use custom icons.

FIGURE 8.8 A long list with list dividers.

LIST DIVIDERS

List dividers let you categorize your list items and are another useful addition to basic linked lists. For example, you could alphabetize your list items and use dividers to group them by letter of the alphabet, or use dividers to group a list of music-related items by genre. The following example shows a list of bands as dividers and some of each band's album titles:

```
<ul data-role="listview">
    <li data-role="list-divider">The Beatles</li>
    <li>Meet The Beatles!</li>
    <li>A Hard Day's Night</li>
    <li>Help!</li>
    <li>Rubber Soul</li>
    <li>Revolver</li>
    <li data-role="list-divider">The Doors</li>
    <li>The Doors</li>
    <li>Strange Days</li>
    <li>Waiting for the Sun</li>
    <li>The Soft Parade</li>
    <li>Morrison Hotel</li>
    <li data-role="list-divider">The Jimi Hendrix Experience</li>
    <li>Are You Experienced</li>
    <li>Bold as Love</li>
    <li>Electric Ladyland</li>
</ul>
```

The highlighted sections in this code example include a data-role with a value of list-divider. Using the data-role attribute value of list-divider visually differentiates these from other list items. **Figure 8.8** shows how the list-divider data-role creates this separation.

COUNT BUBBLES, THUMBNAILS, AND ICONS

You can create different visual styles in your lists with count bubbles, thumbnails, and icons. To add a count bubble to a list item, simply use the ul-li-count class. To separate the count bubble from the list item text, use a span element to contain the count bubble value:

FIGURE 8.9 A simple list with count bubbles.

```
<ul data-role="listview">
    <li>
        <a href="#inbox">Inbox
            <span class="ui-li-count">12</span>
        </a>
    </li>
    <li>
        <a href="#outbox">Outbox
            <span class="ui-li-count">0</span>
        </a>
    </li>
    <li>
        <a href="#sent">Sent
            <span class="ui-li-count">57</span>
        </a>
    </li>
    <li>
        <a href="#trash">Trash
            <span class="ui-li-count">1090</span>
        </a>
    </li>
</ul>
```

The end result of the code in this example is shown in **Figure 8.9**.

Email folders are a good example of list items that can use count bubbles—in this case, to display how many pieces of mail are within each section—but count bubbles can be used for a number of situations. For example, the list divider example with bands and their albums can be converted into a nested list and the parent elements can show how many albums/child list items are in each parent list item:

```
<ul data-role="listview">
    <li>
        <h2>The Beatles</h2>
        <span class="ui-li-count">5</span>
        <ul data-role="listview">
            <li>Meet The Beatles!</li>
            <li>A Hard Day's Night</li>
            <li>Help!</li>
            <li>Rubber Soul</li>
            <li>Revolver</li>
        </ul>
    </li>
    <li>
        <h2>The Doors</h2>
        <span class="ui-li-count">5</span>
        <ul data-role="listview">
            <li>The Doors</li>
            <li>Strange Days</li>
            <li>Waiting for the Sun</li>
            <li>The Soft Parade</li>
            <li>Morrison Hotel</li>
        </ul>
    </li>
```

```
<li>
    <h2>The Jimi Hendrix Experience</h2>
    <span class="ui-li-count">3</span>
    <ul data-role="listview">
        <li>Are You Experienced</li>
        <li>Bold as Love</li>
        <li>Electric Ladyland</li>
    </ul>
</li>
</ul>
```

The result of this example is shown in **Figure 8.10**, with count bubble code and nested lists all in the same list item.

You can add thumbnails just as you would add an image to an HTML page. Simply add an anchor element to a list item, add an image that will act as a thumbnail, and add a title and the text you want to appear next to the icon:

```
<ul data-role="listview">
    <li>
        <a href="#led-zeppelin/led-zeppelin-iv">
            <img src="assets/img/led-zeppelin-IV.png" >
            <h3>Led Zeppelin</h3>
            <p>Led Zeppelin IV</p>
        </a>
    </li>
    <li>
        <a href="#led-zeppelin/houses-of-the-holy">
            <img src="assets/img/houses-of-the-holy.png" >
            <h3>Led Zeppelin</h3>
            <p>Houses of the Holy</p>
```

FIGURE 8.11 A list with list item thumbnails.

```
        </a>
    </li>
</ul>
```

jQuery Mobile knows exactly how to handle lists that are set up this way, as it converts the image into a thumbnail for the list items in the listview immediately. The result of this code is shown in **Figure 8.11**.

Icons are added the same way as thumbnails; the only difference is that you use the ui-li-icon class on the image element:

```
<ul data-role="listview">
    <li>
        <a href="#led-zeppelin/led-zeppelin-iv">
            <img src="assets/img/led-zeppelin-IV.png"
            → class="ui-li-icon" width="16" height="16">
            Led Zeppelin: Led Zeppelin IV
        </a>
    </li>
    <li>
        <a href="#led-zeppelin/houses-of-the-holy">
            <img src="assets/img/houses-of-the-holy.png"
            → class="ui-li-icon" width="16" height="16">
            Led Zeppelin: Houses of the Holy
        </a>
    </li>
</ul>
```

NOTE: width and height have been added to the image tag because there was some overlap with the original images and the text. In a real-world scenario, you should set this width and height with CSS.

The `ul-li-icon` class limits the image size to a maximum width and height of 40 pixels and positions the image properly in the list item. Therefore, the icons you create should fit within these dimensions and, since they are web-based images, they should be set to 72 dpi. The example in **Figure 8.12** shows how this code renders on a mobile device.

WRAPPING **UP**

Lists are of great importance to mobile websites and jQuery Mobile itself. As you've seen in this chapter, the framework relies on lists to create navigation, organize data, and much more. The level of customization is up to you; the options in this chapter can be combined to create the ultimate list.

FIGURE 8.12 A list with list item icons.

9

SEARCH **FILTERING**

Basic search functionality is a common offering on websites these days, but it can be time-consuming to develop. Add to that a search that offers suggestions as the user types, and the development time can double at least. Search suggestions are becoming the norm and people often expect them. Luckily, jQuery Mobile offers a solution: search filtering.

Search filtering is an add-on to the basic `listview`. Adding search filtering is as simple as applying a `data-filter` attribute to an unordered or ordered `listview`. This feature provides great usability improvements for long lists.

CREATING A SEARCH FILTER BAR

As mentioned, the jQuery Mobile framework makes adding a search filter bar to a list incredibly easy: Just add the data-filter attribute to your list and set the value to true. The following example is a truncated list of Beatles songs. Here the data-filter is added to the unordered list element, but it can also be added to ordered lists:

```
<ul data-role="listview" data-filter="true">
    <li>Across The Universe</li>
    <li>Act Naturally</li>
    <li>Ain't She Sweet</li>
    <li>All I've Got To Do</li>
    <li>All My Loving</li>
    <li>All Together Now</li>
    <li>All You Need Is Love</li>
    <li>And I Love Her</li>
    <li>And Your Bird Can Sing</li>
    <li>Anna (Go To Him)</li>
    <li>Another Girl</li>
    <li>Any Time At All</li>
    <li>Ask Me Why</li>
    <li>Baby It's You</li>
    <li>Baby, You're A Rich Man</li>
    <li>Baby's In Black</li>
    <li>Back In The U.S.S.R.</li>
    <li>Bad Boy</li>
    <li>The Ballad Of John And Yoko</li>
    <li>Because</li>
    <li>Being For The Benefit Of Mr. Kite!</li>
    <li>Besame Mucho</li>
    <li>Birthday</li>
    <li>Blackbird</li>
    <!-- etc. -->
</ul>
```

FIGURE 9.1 A basic search filter.

As you can imagine, this list is incredibly long; however, the data-filter attribute adds a search filter bar to the top of the list to help the user find what he's looking for. **Figure 9.1** shows a sample of the sequence of events that happens visually when the user types into the filter field. As letters are typed, the results narrow, revealing only the items that match the search text.

As you can see, the framework adds a default value of "Filter items…" to the search filter input field. You can change this default text with an additional attribute named data-filter-placeholder, which can be used on the opening unordered or ordered list element. The following example shows code that includes this attribute on the previous list of Beatles songs:

```
<ul data-role="listview" data-filter="true"
→ data-filter-placeholder="Search the song list...">
    <li>Across The Universe</li>
    <li>Act Naturally</li>
    <li>Ain't She Sweet</li>
    <li>All I've Got To Do</li>
    <li>All My Loving</li>
    <li>All Together Now</li>
    <li>All You Need Is Love</li>
```

```
<li>And I Love Her</li>
<li>And Your Bird Can Sing</li>
<li>Anna (Go To Him)</li>
<li>Another Girl</li>
<li>Any Time At All</li>
<li>Ask Me Why</li>
<li>Baby It's You</li>
<li>Baby, You're A Rich Man</li>
<li>Baby's In Black</li>
<li>Back In The U.S.S.R.</li>
<li>Bad Boy</li>
<li>The Ballad Of John And Yoko</li>
<li>Because</li>
<li>Being For The Benefit Of Mr. Kite!</li>
<li>Besame Mucho</li>
<li>Birthday</li>
<li>Blackbird</li>
<!-- etc. -->
```
</ul>

The framework lets you change the search filter text through the API. To do this, the listview component must be accessed after mobileinit event is triggered. You'll learn more about the jQuery Mobile API later in the book, but for now it's important to understand that the framework must be initialized before the API can be accessed successfully. Once the listview is accessed, its options can be altered. One such option is the filterPlaceholder property, which can be used to update the search filter text. The following code shows a complete example of how to write the code, including binding to the mobileinit event:

FIGURE 9.2 (Left) A basic search filter with custom placeholder text.

FIGURE 9.3 (Right) A basic search filter on a custom-formatted `listview`.

```
$(document).bind("mobileinit", function() {

    $.mobile.listview.prototype.options.filterPlaceholder =
    →  "Search the song list...";

});
```

Both of these options have the same visual result, allowing you to define any text you want to appear in the search field. **Figure 9.2** shows an example of how the search filter looks with custom placeholder text.

Another nice feature of the search filter bar is that you can filter not only a basic listview, but also a listview that includes custom formatting. A search filter on a custom formatted list actually searches all the text within each list item, whether it's titles, paragraphs, or something else—you name it, the framework will filter it. **Figure 9.3** shows an example sequence of a custom formatted listview with a search filter. The results include list items with a combination of matching text from the paragraph copy and titles.

CREATING **CUSTOM** SEARCH **FILTERS**

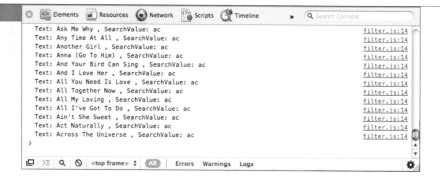

FIGURE 9.4 The search filter as it loops through list items looking for matching text strings.

The jQuery Mobile framework gives you two options for creating custom search filters. The `listview` includes a `filterCallback` option that can be extended with a custom callback function. By extending this callback function, two arguments—text and searchValue—become available and can be used to write custom search criteria. The text argument is the value of the current list item, while the searchValue is the value of the text that's typed into the search filter. As a user types into the search filter, the `listview` loops through the list comparing the list item text and the search value, and filtering the results as necessary. **Figure 9.4** shows an example of a console.log as jQuery Mobile compares the search value and each list item's text.

To customize the criteria, you can simply set a callback function using the `filterCallback` property:

```
$.mobile.listview.prototype.options.filterCallback =
→ myCustomCallback;
```

Or, you can access a specific `listview` by id and set the `filterCallback` property for that `listview` only:

```
$('#my-listview').listview('option', 'filterCallback',
→ myCustomCallback);
```

Let's try adding a custom search filter to the Beatles song list using the `listview` function. First, we'll add a `pageinit` event to ensure that the page has loaded and that it's been enhanced by the framework. To do so we'll need to add an id to the page so we can target it with jQuery. The following example shows a page with an id that can be targeted. A custom JavaScript file called filter.js is the file we'll use to create the callback function:

```html
<!DOCTYPE html>
<html>
<head>
    <meta http-equiv="Content-Type" content="text/html;
    → charset=UTF-8">
    <meta name="viewport" content="width=device-width,
    → initial-scale=1">
    <title>List view - jQuery Mobile: Design and Develop</title>
    <link rel="stylesheet" href="http://code.jquery.com/
    → mobile/1.0.1/jquery.mobile-1.0.1.min.css" />
    <script src="http://ajax.googleapis.com/ajax/libs/jquery/1.7.1/
    → jquery.min.js"></script>
    <script src="assets/js/filter.js"></script>
    <script src="http://code.jquery.com/mobile/1.0.1/
    → jquery.mobile-1.0.1.min.js"></script>
</head>
<body>
    <div data-role="page" id="beatles-page">
        <div data-role="header">
            <h1>The Beatles</h1>
        </div>
        <div data-role="content">
            <ul data-role="listview" data-filter="true">
                <li>Across The Universe</li>
                <li>Act Naturally</li>
                <li>Ain't She Sweet</li>
                <li>All I've Got To Do</li>
                <li>All My Loving</li>
                <li>All Together Now</li>
                <li>All You Need Is Love</li>
```

```
                    <li>And I Love Her</li>

                    <li>And Your Bird Can Sing</li>

                    <li>Anna (Go To Him)</li>

                    <li>Another Girl</li>

                    <li>Any Time At All</li>

                    <li>Ask Me Why</li>

                    <li>Baby It's You</li>

                    <li>Baby, You're A Rich Man</li>

                    <li>Baby's In Black</li>

                    <li>Back In The U.S.S.R.</li>

                    <li>Bad Boy</li>

                    <li>The Ballad Of John And Yoko</li>

                    <li>Because</li>

                    <li>Being For The Benefit Of Mr. Kite!</li>

                    <li>Besame Mucho</li>

                    <li>Birthday</li>

                    <li>Blackbird</li>

                <!-- etc. -->

            </ul>

    </body>

    </html>
```

Once we have an `id` for the `listview` and have included a custom JavaScript file, we can target the `listview` from within the JavaScript file. First, the document must be ready. Once the document is ready, an event handler is created for the `pageinit` method for the `beatles-page` element. When the page is initialized, the `listview` code is executed, and the `defaultSearch` function is used as the custom callback function:

```
$(document).ready(function() {
    $('div#beatles-page').on({
```

```
        pageinit: function(event) {
            $('#beatles-listview').listview('option',
            → 'filterCallback', defaultSearch);

        }
    });
});
function defaultSearch( text, searchValue ) {
    console.log("Text: "+ text, ", SearchValue: "+ searchValue);
    return text.toLowerCase().indexOf( searchValue ) === -1;
};
```

This example uses the default search criteria to log the text and searchValue for testing purposes. Minus the console.log, this is the exact code that jQuery Mobile uses to filter results as they're entered into the search filter bar. First, the text is converted to lowercase to make it a case-insensitive search, then JavaScript's native indexOf function looks for a string matching the searchValue in the text.

Now let's take a look at how a custom callback function can be coded. This time we'll use the custom formatted listview from the earlier example and apply a filter to it that searches only the body copy, excluding the list item titles from the search criteria:

```
$(document).bind("mobileinit", function() {
    $.mobile.listview.prototype.options.filterCallback = onlyBody;
});
function onlyBody( text, searchValue ) {
    var splitText = text.trim().split("\n");
    console.log("text: "+ splitText[1]);
    return splitText[1].toLowerCase().indexOf( searchValue ) === -1;
};
String.prototype.trim = function() {
    return this.replace(/^\s+|\s+$/g,"");
}
```

In this example, we need only wait for the `mobileinit` event, because the `filterCallback` property for all `listviews` is accessible before the jQuery Mobile framework enhances the markup for the page. (In the previous example, the specific `listview` we were targeting had to be enhanced by the framework before it could be accessed.) Once the `mobileinit` event is triggered, we'll set the `filterCallback` to `onlyBody`, a custom callback function that can be structured like any other, but it will receive two arguments, `text` and `searchValue`. With these arguments we can write any rules we desire. In this case, we'll split the `text` argument and match results only for the body copy that was included in the p element from the earlier custom formatted list example.

In addition to creating custom filter callback functions, jQuery Mobile also offers an attribute named `data-filtertext` for filtering list items. The interesting thing about this attribute is that it will actually be the text value that's sent to the `filterCallback` function. In other words, the value in the `data-filtertext` attribute becomes the value that the `filterCallback` function uses during comparison:

```
<ul data-role="listview" data-filter="true">
    <li data-filtertext="AL">Alabama</li>
    <li data-filtertext="AK">Alaska</li>
    <li data-filtertext="AZ">Arizona</li>
    <li data-filtertext="AR">Arkansas</li>
    <li data-filtertext="CA">California</li>
    <li data-filtertext="CO">Colorado</li>
    <li data-filtertext="CT">Connecticut</li>
    <li data-filtertext="DE">Delaware</li>
</ul>
```

FIGURE 9.5 With a data-filtertext attribute applied, the search criteria can be different from the actual list item values.

The markup in this example uses the `data-filtertext` attribute to filter a list by state abbreviation rather than the full state name value of the list items. **Figure 9.5** shows how this filter works; typing "ar" would usually result in "Arizona" and "Arkansas," but since this list is being filtered by state abbreviation, "Arkansas" is the only match.

WRAPPING **UP**

Search filter bars offer capabilities that would otherwise be rather complex and time-consuming to program. jQuery Mobile makes it incredibly easy to add and even customize this functionality. In addition to saving time, this widget provides added value to any large amount of data and offers great usability enhancements, helping users find what they're looking for quickly and efficiently. Sometimes it's just not possible to pare down all the content that needs to go on a mobile website. When this is the case and you have a very long list that seems nearly unusable, the search filter bar is a great way to handle the problem.

10

FORM **ELEMENTS**

The jQuery Mobile framework has exposed a number of internal methods and events for each form element, which means that you can access them from your custom code. These methods and events let you alter and extend core jQuery Mobile form element functionality to create customizations that set your mobile application apart from the rest. This chapter covers each of the exposed form element methods and events that are available to you.

TEXT **INPUTS**

FIGURE 10.1 A numeric keyboard is revealed when using the number element type.

FIGURE 10.2 A telephone keypad for number patterns.

jQuery Mobile supports many different text input types, including HTML5 inputs, such as number, e-mail, URL, phone, and a few time- and date-related inputs. The framework enhances all form elements to make them more usable on mobile devices. One major advantage to identifying form elements with a specific element type is that the keyboard changes. Following are some examples of the different text inputs and the associated iOS keyboards after they've been enhanced by jQuery Mobile.

Setting an element type is done by adding an attribute named type and setting its value to any of the values listed in this section. Here's an example of a text input with the type set to number:

```
<input type="number" name="number">
```

When the element type is set to number, the input forces iOS to display a numeric keyboard (**Figure 10.1**).

When the element type is set to number, but includes a pattern attribute of 0–9, the telephone pad appears (**Figure 10.2**).

To use a number pattern, simply append a `pattern` attribute and define the pattern. The pattern used in this example allows any number between 0 and 9 to be entered into this number field. This pattern is based on a regular expression. You can find more information about regular expressions at regexpal.com; you can also use the site to test the regular expressions you write:

```
<input type="number" name="number" pattern="[0-9]*"
  id="number-pattern">
```

When the element type is set to `email`, iOS includes an alphabetical keyboard with an @ symbol and a period to help speed up input. If you have other mobile devices, you can easily set up a form with these input types to see how each keyboard responds (**Figure 10.3**).

FIGURE 10.3 An alphabetical keyboard with an @ symbol and a period for e-mail addresses.

jQUERY MOBILE 1.1.0

Just prior to publication of this book, a new version of the jQuery Mobile framework, version 1.1.0 final, was released. To benefit from some of the new form element options, you must use the following code when including the framework, CSS, and jQuery in your pages:

```
<link rel="stylesheet" href="http://code.jquery.com/mobile/1.1.0/
  jquery.mobile-1.1.0.min.css" />
```

```
<script src="http://ajax.googleapis.com/ajax/libs/jquery/1.7.1/
  jquery.min.js"></script>
```

```
<script src="http://code.jquery.com/mobile/1.1.0/
  jquery.mobile-1.1.0.min.js"></script>
```

The jQuery Mobile framework is constantly being upgraded. Check the download page on jquerymobile.com before starting a project to ensure you have the latest and greatest code.

FIGURE 10.4 An alphabetical keyboard with a forward slash and .com key for URLs.

FIGURE 10.6 The time- and date-related menus in iOS.

FIGURE 10.5 A telephone keypad for phone numbers.

A url element type reveals an alphabetical keyboard with a forward slash and a .com key (**Figure 10.4**).

A tel element type reveals a telephone keypad for phone numbers (**Figure 10.5**).

The time, month, date, and datetime element types all reveal a menu that corresponds with the appropriate value (**Figure 10.6**).

OPTIONS

Text inputs include two options: initSelector and theme. Both are available when accessing textinput through the $.mobile object. The following code shows how to access the options through the textinput:

```
$.mobile.textinput.prototype.options
```

Once you have access to the options, you can access each of them individually. For example, if you want the initSelector option, you can append the option to the end of the previous line of code:

```
$.mobile.textinput.prototype.options.initSelector
```

The initSelector option defines the selectors that are initialized when the framework is initialized. The fact that this option is exposed is what lets you define what selectors you want initialized as text inputs. This gives you great control over core functionality, allowing you to define what is initialized based on your specific situation, which ultimately minimizes initialization time. Not only can you define what element types are initialized, you can do the same for data roles. The following code leaves out all number element types as textinputs:

```
$( document ).bind("mobileinit", function() {
    $.mobile.textinput.prototype.options.initSelector =
    → "input[type='text'], input[type='search'],
    → :jqmData(type='search'), input[type='password'],
    → input[type='email'], input[type='url'], input[type='tel'],
    → textarea, input:not([type])";
});
```

> **NOTE:** A number of different element types can be created with the textinput element in jQuery Mobile, including text, search, number, password, email, url, and tel. In addition to these, the textarea is grouped into the textinput form element category in jQuery Mobile. This means that each element type includes the options, methods, and events in the text input section of this chapter.

FIGURE 10.7 A number element without enhancements from the jQuery Mobile framework.

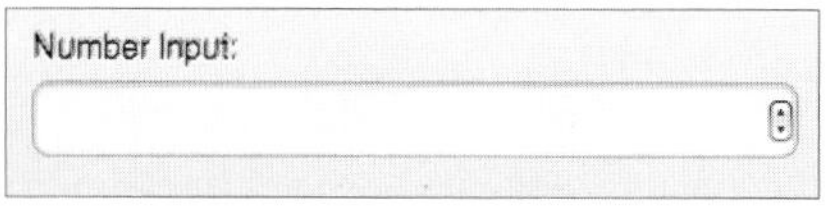

FIGURE 10.8 A number element with enhancements from the jQuery Mobile framework.

FIGURE 10.9 Regular and mini text inputs.

Figure 10.7 shows an example of the number element type without the enhancements.

With the enhancements, the number element looks much nicer and is easier for users to interact with in a mobile environment (**Figure 10.8**).

The textinput also includes a theme option, which you can access when selecting a text input element. The value of the theme can be set based on any prebuilt or custom swatch that includes a–z:

```
$('.my-textinput').textinput({theme: 'a'});
```

This example accesses a text input element with a class name of .my-textinput and sets the theme to a. You'll learn more about themes in the next chapter.

As of version 1.1.0, jQuery Mobile also includes two new options: mini and preventFocusZoom. These can also be set on an individual form element by using the data- attribute named mini. Setting a form element to mini creates a more compact version of it. To set a form element to mini with code, simply select the text input(s), then use the textinput method to set the value of mini:

```
$('.my-textinput').textinput({mini: true});
```

The result of this code on a text input looks similar to the right input in **Figure 10.9**, which shows a comparison of the regular and mini text inputs.

FIGURE 10.10 A disabled text input element.

The final option in the text input is the preventFocusZoom Boolean. When set to true in iOS only, this option prevents the webpage from becoming zoomed in when a user selects a text input. This is not the default: Usually iOS zooms the webpage into the input, providing complete focus on the form element. This behavior is often unnecessary, so luckily the jQuery Mobile team has provided an option for disabling it. You can also set this option on an individual form element by using the data- attribute named prevent-focus-zoom:

```
$('.my-textinput').textinput({preventFocusZoom: true});
```

In addition to these options, the search input in particular has a specific option called clearSearchButtonText that can be used to clear the search input text. Simply set it as we've done with previous options:

```
$('.my-textinput').textinput({clearSearchButtonText: 'this can be
→ any custom text'});
```

METHODS

jQuery Mobile exposes two simple methods for the textinput element: enable and disable. The enable method activates the input and lets the user enter the text input and type in it:

```
$('.my-textinput').textinput('enable');
```

When a text input is disabled, the user can't interact with it:

```
$('.my-textinput').textinput('disable');
```

We've already seen an enabled text input in Figure 10.8; a disabled element looks like **Figure 10.10**.

EVENTS

Text inputs can also be bound with virtual events or standard JavaScript events. JavaScript events that can be bound to a text input include focus, blur, and change. Virtual events are covered later in the book and include vmouseover, vmousedown, vmousemove, vmouseup, vclick, and vmousecancel. These events are more relevant to mobile devices that don't include a mouse. To bind an event to a text input, simply use the bind method, include the event that you're binding, and tie it to a function handler:

```
$(".my-textinput").bind("change", function(event, ui) {
    console.log('my-textinput has changed');
});
```

jQuery Mobile also adds custom events to some form elements. The text input includes a create event as its custom event. The create event can be used to execute custom code when a text input is created.

```
$(".my-textinput").textinput({
    create: function(event, ui) {
        console.log('my-textinput has been created');
    }
});
```

CHECKBOXES AND RADIO BUTTONS

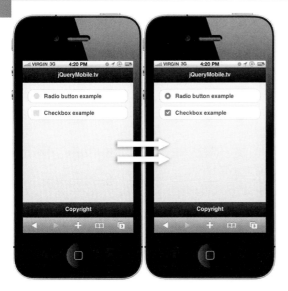

FIGURE 10.11 The layout and sequence from selecting a radio button and checkbox.

Checkboxes and radio buttons are similar in their options and markup. The main difference is that you can select only a single radio button from a group. However, you can select one, many, or all checkboxes in a group. Each element type has the same layout options. For example, when you add a label and a checkbox or a label and a radio button, you'll receive the label and the element embedded in a button:

```
<label for="my-radio">Radio button example</label>

<input type="radio" name="name" id="my-radio" class="my-radio" />

<label for="my-checkbox">Checkbox example</label>

<input type="checkbox" name="name" id="my-checkbox"
→ class="my-checkbox" />
```

The result of this code can be seen in **Figure 10.11**.

To add a question or statement to a group of radio buttons or checkboxes, you can use the legend element. To group a legend with input elements, you can use a fieldset with a data-role of controlgroup. Lastly, surrounding the fieldset element div with a data-role of fieldcontain adds some styling, such as a margin and a bottom border, to the elements in this group of pizza ingredients:

```
<div data-role="fieldcontain">
    <fieldset data-role="controlgroup">
        <legend>Pizza ingredients:</legend>
        <label for="cheese">Cheese</label>
        <input type="checkbox" name="pizza-ingredients" id="cheese"
        → value="cheese" />
        <label for="mushroom">Mushroom</label>
        <input type="checkbox" name="pizza-ingredients"
        → id="mushroom" value="mushroom" />
        <label for="pepperoni">Pepperoni</label>
        <input type="checkbox" name="pizza-ingredients"
        → id="pepperoni" value="pepperoni" />
        <label for="green-pepper">Green Pepper</label>
        <input type="checkbox" name="pizza-ingredients"
        → id="green-pepper" value="green-pepper" />
    </fieldset>
</div>
```

FIGURE 10.12 A group of input elements with a legend in a fieldset.

The controlgroup data-role groups the buttons visually as shown in **Figure 10.12**.

It's also possible to create what's called a horizontal toggle set. This groups elements and reveals them only as text options, rather than including the actual radio button or checkbox icon. To create a toggle set, add a data-type of horizontal to the fieldset. The following markup is a good example of when and why you would use this type of format:

```
<div data-role="fieldcontain">
    <fieldset data-role="controlgroup" data-type="horizontal">
        <legend>Font styles:</legend>
        <label for="bold" class="bold">b</label>
        <input type="checkbox" name="font-style" id="bold"
        → value="bold" />
        <label for="italic" class="italic">i</label>
        <input type="checkbox" name="font-style" id="italic"
        → value="italic" />
        <label for="underline" class="underline">u</label>
        <input type="checkbox" name="font-style" id="underline"
        → value="underline" />
    </fieldset>
</div>
```

FIGURE 10.13 A group of buttons with horizontal toggle set formatting.

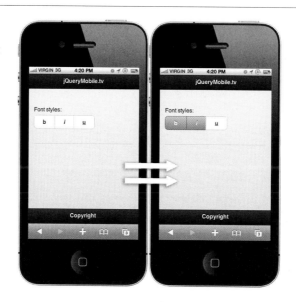

This format provides button-like functionality that can be toggled, in this case to turn font styles on and off. This code would not be complete without some CSS formatting; in this case, the following CSS will be applied to the labels:

```
<style type="text/css">
.bold {
    font-weight: bold;
}
.italic {
    font-style: oblique;
}
.underline {
    text-decoration: underline;
}
</style>
```

The result of this code looks similar to **Figure 10.13**.

Checkboxes and radio buttons are simpler than text inputs in that they have only a theme and mini option, both of which are also available as data- attributes. Neither element can include different types; the element type is either checkbox or radio, so there's no need for an initSelector. Setting the theme for a checkbox or radio button is similar to setting the theme for a text input. The main difference is that you need to access the checkboxradio, rather than the textinput. The following code sets the theme for all checkbox and radio buttons and makes them all mini:

```
$("input[type='checkbox'], input[type='radio']").checkboxradio({
        mini: "true",
        theme: "e"
});
```

In terms of methods, checkboxes and radio buttons both have the standard enable and disable methods. However, they also include a refresh method, which you can use to update an element after visually manipulating it. For example, if we took the pizza ingredients example and wanted to preselect cheese as an ingredient choice, we could use the following code with a refresh:

```
$("input#cheese").attr("checked", true).checkboxradio("refresh");
```

This method ensures that the visual update is made to the checkbox, so the user sees the checkbox as selected.

The checkbox and radio button elements include the same events as the text input. These include the ability to bind standard JavaScript events, such as a change, blur, focus event, and so on. These elements also have a create event that you can use to execute custom code when they're created in jQuery Mobile.

SELECT **MENUS**

FIGURE 10.14 An action sequence of a select menu.

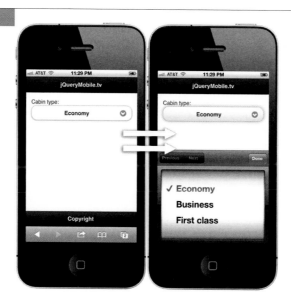

Select menus have been notoriously difficult to visually adjust. Finally, jQuery Mobile has provided a visual look that makes sense with the framework and requires no additional custom CSS coding. To create a select menu for jQuery Mobile, create a regular HTML select menu. The following example shows a simple select menu to choose a cabin type for a flight:

```
<label for="select-cabin">Cabin type:</label>
<select name="select-cabin" id="select-cabin">
    <option value="economy">Economy</option>
    <option value="business">Business</option>
    <option value="first">First class</option>
</select>
```

The result of this markup looks and functions like the example shown in **Figure 10.14**.

FIGURE 10.15 A select menu in a `fieldcontain`.

As with checkboxes and radio buttons, you can add a bit of formatting. The following example includes a div with the `fieldcontain` data-role, which formats the label and select menu slightly differently (**Figure 10.15**):

```
<div data-role="fieldcontain">
    <label for="select-cabin">Cabin type:</label>
    <select name="select-cabin" id="select-cabin">
        <option value="economy">Economy</option>
        <option value="business">Business</option>
        <option value="first">First class</option>
    </select>
</div>
```

The result of this markup looks and functions like **Figure 10.15**.

You can also group select menus as we did with checkboxes and radio buttons. Simply add the `controlgroup` data-role to a `fieldset` and create a legend for the group of menus:

```
<div data-role="fieldcontain">
    <fieldset data-role="controlgroup">
        <legend>Flight details:</legend>
        <label for="select-cabin">Cabin type:</label>
        <select name="select-cabin" id="select-cabin">
            <option>Cabin type</option>
            <option value="economy">Economy</option>
            <option value="business">Business</option>
            <option value="first">First class</option>
        </select>
        <label for="select-adults">Adults</label>
        <select name="select-adults" id="select-adults">
            <option>Adults</option>
            <option value="1">1</option>
            <option value="2">2</option>
            <!-- etc. -->
        </select>
        <label for="select-time">Time</label>
```

FIGURE 10.16 (Left) A select menu in a controlgroup.

FIGURE 10.17 (Right) Horizontally grouped select menus.

```
      <select name="select-time" id="select-time">
          <option>Time</option>
          <option value="6">6:00AM</option>
          <option value="7">7:00AM</option>
          <!-- etc. -->
      </select>
  </fieldset>
</div>
```

The result of this markup looks similar to **Figure 10.16**.

Or, this group can be a horizontal group of select inputs, which works well for items that are only a few characters long, such as a date of birth (**Figure 10.17**).

OPTIONS

You can also do quite a bit of customization on the select menu using options via the API or as data- attribute counterparts. The options that can be set for a select menu are shown in **Table 10.1**. All of these options can be set via the `selectmenu` method, except the `initSelector` option, which is set the same way as a text input.

TABLE 10.1 Select menu options

OPTION	DESCRIPTION
corners	A Boolean used to apply the border-radius to the select button. The default is true.
icon	A string that can be set to any of the built-in icons or a custom icon. The default is "arrow-down".
iconpos	A string used to set the position of an icon, if one is used. The default is "right".
iconshadow	A Boolean used to apply a shadow to the select button. The default is true.
initSelector	A string that lets you change which elements are initialized by jQuery Mobile. Aside from the actual select menu itself, the only other option is a data-role for the slider element.
inline	A Boolean used to make the select button act like an inline button, which means that the width is determined by the button's text value. The default is false.
mini	A Boolean that creates a more compact version of the select menu, just as it does other form elements. The default is false.
nativeMenu	A Boolean that can be set to determine whether the native menu for the device is used when the select button is selected. The default for this option is true, as can be seen in the figures that feature the select menu in iOS throughout this section.
overlayTheme	A theme can be defined for the overlay layer of the select menu. The default is a.
preventFocusZoom	A Boolean used to prevent or allow the device to zoom into the select menu when it is selected. The default is true on iOS platforms.
shadow	A Boolean that applies a shadow to the select button. The default is true.
theme	A theme that can be associated with the select menu. This option's default value is inherited from its parent.

METHODS

A select menu has more functionality than a text input, checkbox, or radio button and therefore has more methods associated with it. The standard enable and disable methods are included, but this element also includes close, open, and refresh. refresh can be used when a select menu has been rebuilt, for example, if Ajax were used to update the select menu based on prior selections in a web form. Or, this method can be used to refresh the menu if a visual update has been made. The open and close methods are self-explanatory, but here's an example of how to use the open method:

```
$('select').selectmenu('open');
```

This code would set all select menus to open by default.

We've already covered all the select menu events. This form element includes the option to be bound to standard JavaScript events and includes a create event.

SLIDERS

FIGURE 10.18 An example of a basic slider.

Sliders are a great addition to the group of form elements that are available for enhancement via jQuery Mobile. A slider can be used to choose a number within a certain range as it sets that number in a corresponding number input. To create a slider, you must set the element type to range and include a min and max value:

```
<label for="my-slider">My slider</label>

<input type="range" name="slider" id="my-slider" value="50" min="0"
→ max="100" />
```

A default value can also be added, which sets the position of the handle on the track. The slider in this example displays like **Figure 10.18**.

You can also add steps to the values that are returned. For example, if you didn't want to return every single number between 0 and 100, you could set the step attribute to 10, which would return every tenth number:

```
<label for="my-slider">My slider</label>

<input type="range" name="slider" id="my-slider" value="50" min="0"
→ max="100" step="10" />
```

FIGURE 10.19 A slider with a fill highlight.

In addition to these attributes, you can add a fill highlight, which highlights the area of the track to the left of the handle (**Figure 10.19**):

```
<label for="my-slider">My slider</label>
<input type="range" name="slider" id="my-slider" value="50" min="0"
→ max="100" step="10" data-highlight="true" />
```

OPTIONS

The slider element has a decent selection of options you can set via the API or as data-role attributes, including disabled, highlight, initSelector, mini, theme, and trackTheme. By default, the disabled option is set to false. The highlight option defaults to false; however, it can be used to highlight the track to the left of the handle on all sliders if set to true, as in the following example:

```
$('.selector').slider({ highlight: "true" });
```

We've already covered the initSelector, mini, and theme options. The trackTheme option is unique to the slider; you can use it to set the theme of the track to a different theme than the rest of the slider.

METHODS AND EVENTS

The slider plug-in includes three methods you can use to modify a `slider` element: enable, disable, and refresh. The enable method enables a disabled slider:

```
$('.selector').slider('enable');
```

The `disable` method disables a slider so the user can't interact with it:

```
$('.selector').slider('disable');
```

The `refresh` method can be used to refresh a slider after it's been updated visually or functionally via JavaScript:

```
$('.selector').slider('refresh');
```

The events available to the slider plug-in are similar to those for other form elements. They include the ability to be bound to any standard JavaScript event, such as change, focus, blur, and so on. The slider plug-in also includes a create event you can use to execute custom code when the slider is created.

FLIP TOGGLE SWITCHES

Flip toggle switches are another handy addition to the mobile form element lineup. They provide a great solution for binary data, such as yes/no, on/off, or true/false functionality. The switch can be dragged from one position to another or the user can press the option and the switch will flip to the selected location. It's easy to make a flip toggle switch: simply create a slider with only two options. The options can be anything you like, of any length, because the control resizes proportionally to accommodate the text:

```
<label for="flip-switch">Do you like pizza?</label>
<select name="slider" id="flip-switch" data-role="slider">
    <option value="yes">Yes</option>
    <option value="no">No</option>
</select>
```

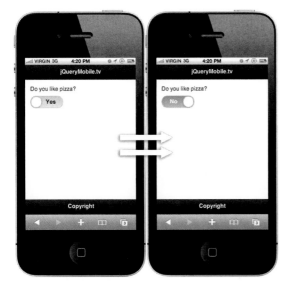

FIGURE 10.20 A toggle switch interaction sequence.

The code that produces this toggle switch is a select menu with a `data-role` set to a value of `slider` and, of course, the key is to include only two options. The visual result of this slider is shown in **Figure 10.20**.

The flip toggle switch includes the exact same options, methods, and events as the slider, and each is accessed with the same syntax since the flip toggle switch is essentially just an extension of the slider. To learn more about the options, methods, and events accessible to the flip toggle switch, check out the "Sliders" section earlier in this chapter.

WRAPPING **UP**

jQuery Mobile offers great element options for handling form input. Usability increases dramatically with devices that respond with the appropriate keyboard based on the input type. Another bonus is that all of these form elements degrade when viewed in a browser that can't handle them, so you never need to worry about your webpage breaking because someone isn't using the latest and greatest mobile phone, for example. This is just another way that jQuery Mobile helps eliminate some of the common frustrations that come along with web development in general.

11

THEMING
jQUERY MOBILE

jQuery Mobile includes a complete theme framework that lets you customize color swatches and icon sets to create custom themed pages, toolbars, content, form elements, lists, buttons, and more. The framework uses CSS3 for many of its enhancements, such as shadows, gradients, and rounded corners, so no images are used to make these visual aspects, which makes the theme more lightweight and quick loading.

This chapter provides an overview of the existing color swatches as well as details on how to create a custom theme. Custom theming allows you to create mobile versions of websites that follow the same branding as desktop versions, creating a unified design between your websites.

jQuery Mobile has a theme system containing five swatches that are defined by the letters "a" through "e." Swatches can be mixed and matched throughout a single webpage to allow for complete customization. The default swatches all contain color and texture, padding, and predefined dimensions to separate them from one another. **Table 11.1** includes the default swatches and descriptions of each.

TABLE 11.1 jQuery Mobile default swatches

SWATCH	COLOR	PRIORITY
a	Black	Highest
b	Blue	Secondary
c	Gray	Baseline
d	White	Alternate secondary
e	Yellow	Accent

FIGURE 11.1 Group of buttons with different theme swatches assigned.

Using a swatch is as simple as using the `data-theme` attribute, which can be used on any HTML element with the jQuery Mobile framework. The following code shows a group of five buttons, each with a different default theme:

```
<a href="#" data-role="button" data-theme="a">Swatch A</a>

<a href="#" data-role="button" data-theme="b">Swatch B</a>

<a href="#" data-role="button" data-theme="c">Swatch C</a>

<a href="#" data-role="button" data-theme="d">Swatch D</a>

<a href="#" data-role="button" data-theme="e">Swatch E</a>
```

Whether this is a set of buttons, list items, or bars, the jQuery Mobile framework gives you the ability to define different themes for these items. **Figure 11.1** shows the group of buttons in the example. As you can see, each has a different color based on the theme assigned to it.

You can update an existing swatch or create a custom color swatch. To create a custom swatch, simply copy an existing theme swatch from the jQuery Mobile style sheet and update it to a letter that's not already in use as a default swatch (that is, letters "f" through "z" or any custom name). First, you'll need to find a swatch in the style sheet that you want to copy; let's use the "a" swatch for this example. The style sheet that we want to get the swatch from is the one that we've been attaching to all the samples throughout this book. The only difference here is that we'll look at the non-minified version to make it easier to find where the swatch begins and ends. You'll find the non-minified version of this style sheet at http://code.jquery.com/mobile/1.0.1/jquery.mobile-1.0.1.css, which is the same address we've been including all along, minus the .*min* portion in the CSS's filename. To create a copy of the swatch simply copy and paste the many CSS swatch classes into a new CSS file and do a search and replace on the suffix "-a", with a letter between "f" and "z." For example, to create an "f" swatch, you would search and replace "-a" with "-f" and all the CSS swatch classes would be updated, leaving you with a new "f" swatch. Here's an example of the ui-bar class after it's been modified for the "f" swatch:

```
.ui-bar-f {
    border: 1px solid #cccccc;
    background: #cccccc;
    color: #cccccc;
    font-weight: bold;
    text-shadow: 0 -1px 1px #000000;
    background-image: -webkit-gradient(linear, left top,
    → left bottom, from(#cccccc), to(#999));
    background-image: -webkit-linear-gradient(#cccccc, #999);
    background-image:    -moz-linear-gradient(#cccccc, #999);
    background-image:     -ms-linear-gradient(#cccccc, #999);
    background-image:      -o-linear-gradient(#cccccc, #999);
    background-image:         linear-gradient(#cccccc, #999);
}
```

Now it's up to you to customize the properties of those classes. Once you have your new swatch, you can easily use it on any jQuery Mobile element, as in the following button example:

```
<a href="#" data-role="button" data-theme="f">Custom Swatch F</a>
```

THE **THEMEROLLER**

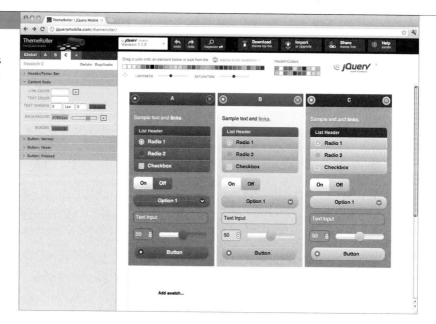

FIGURE 11.2 Custom swatches in a custom theme made with the ThemeRoller tool.

Another way to create a custom swatch is to use the ThemeRoller tool, which lets you create an entire theme with multiple custom swatches in a simple interface.

TIP: The ThemeRoller tool is an easy way to create a custom theme, but the tougher route can give you a better understanding of the inner workings of the CSS classes that are applied when the jQuery mobile framework enhances your markup. Even if you ultimately use the ThemeRoller tool, it's a good idea to check out the existing classes to see what's happening behind the scenes.

The ThemeRoller is a drag-and-drop interface that allows you to drag color blocks to customize swatches. The tool starts you out with three swatches that are represented with a few components. At the top, there are color blocks that you can drag and drop to headers, buttons, text, backgrounds, links, and more. Then, you can get more detailed with your customizations in the left sidebar, where you can set fonts, shadows, rounded corners, icons, and so on. **Figure 11.2** shows an example of three swatches that were customized with the drag-and-drop interface.

These are a few simple and somewhat unattractive examples, but you can get much more detailed by spending more time with the tool. To get started using the ThemeRoller, visit www.jquerymobile.com/themeroller.

THEMING **COMPONENTS**

Each component handles theme swatches in its own way. This section provides an overview of how each component handles swatches and gives you a visual reference.

PAGE, TOOLBAR, AND BUTTON THEMING

Theming pages is a great way to style an entire page, because the page theme is inherited by all internal components. For example, if the page theme is set to the "a" swatch, then any component placed within the page inherits the "a" swatch. Of course, this can be overridden, but it provides a great baseline for the entire page, allowing customizations to occur only when necessary. Any div or element that includes a data-role of page receives a default theme. The following markup is an example of a page with the data-theme set to the "b" swatch:

FIGURE 11.3 The "b" swatch applied to the page component.

```
<div data-role="page" data-theme="b">

    <div data-role="header"><h1>jQueryMobile.tv</h1></div>

    <div data-role="content">

        <h3>Header</h3>

        <p>This is a sample with the "b" swatch applied to the page.
        → As you can see, the header and footer are defaulting to
        → the "a" theme, while the rest of the page is set to the
        → "b" theme. To change this you must apply the "b" swatch
        → directly to the header and footer components.</p>

        <a href="#" data-role="button" data-inline="true">Button</a>

    </div>

    <div data-role="footer"><h2>Copyright</h2></div>

</div>
```

Figure 11.3 shows an example of this markup in action.

FIGURE 11.4 The "b" swatch applied to the page component and header and footer toolbars.

FIGURE 11.5 A toolbar component with a button that has a different data-theme swatch.

As you can see, the header and footer default to the "a" theme, while the rest of the page is set to the "b" theme. To change this, you must apply the "b" swatch directly to the header and footer components:

```
<div data-role="page" data-theme="b">

    <div data-role="header" data-theme="b"><h1>jQueryMobile.tv</h1>
    → </div>

    <div data-role="content">

        <h3>Header</h3>

        <p>This is a sample with the "b" swatch applied to the page.
        → As you can see, the header and footer are defaulting to
        → the "a" theme, while the rest of the page is set to the
        → "b" theme. To change this you must apply the "b" swatch
        → directly to the header and footer components.</p>

        <a href="#" data-role="button" data-inline="true">Button</a>

    </div>

    <div data-role="footer" data-theme="b"><h2>Copyright</h2></div>

</div>
```

Figure 11.4 shows the result of this modified markup with the data-theme.

Like pages, any components included in the toolbar inherit the toolbar's theme. The following example shows a header with a button that has a different theme and the home icon:

```
<div data-role="header" data-theme="b">

    <h1>jQueryMobile.tv</h1>

    <a href="#" data-theme="e" data-icon="home">Home</a>

</div>
```

This markup creates a button that stands out against the toolbar theme (**Figure 11.5**).

CONTENT THEMING

The main content area or any element that includes a data-role of content can be themed by adding a data-theme attribute. This allows the content area to override the inherited page component's theme for itself and its components. The following example shows how the content theme, as well as any component it contains, can override the page theme:

```
<div data-role="page" data-theme="b">

    <div data-role="header" data-theme="b">

        <h1>jQueryMobile.tv</h1>

        <a href="#" data-theme="e" data-icon="home">Home</a>

    </div>

    <div data-role="content" data-theme="d">

        <h3>Header</h3>

        <p>This is a sample with the "b" swatch applied to the page
        → and toolbars and the "d" swatch applied to the content
        → area.</p>

        <a href="#" data-role="button" data-inline="true">Button</a>

    </div>

    <div data-role="footer" data-theme="b"><h2>Copyright</h2></div>

</div>
```

FIGURE 11.6 A page with a content area that has a different theme than itself.

Notice how the page uses the "b" swatch, while the content area uses the "d" swatch. **Figure 11.6** shows how the content component and its components override the inherited page component theme.

In addition to a standard content area, the collapsible content area can include a custom theme to differentiate it from its parent:

FIGURE 11.7 A page with a collapsible content area.

```
<div data-role="page" data-theme="b">
    <div data-role="header" data-theme="b">
        <h1>jQueryMobile.tv</h1>
        <a href="#" data-theme="e" data-icon="home">Home</a>
    </div>
    <div data-role="content" data-theme="d">
        <h3>Header</h3>
        <p>This is a sample with the "b" swatch applied to the page
        → and toolbars and the "d" swatch applied to the content
        → area.</p>
        <div data-role="collapsible" data-collapsed="true"
        → data-theme="c" data-content-theme="c">
            <h3>Collapsible header</h3>
            <p>I use the data-content-theme to match my header</p>
        </div>
    </div>
    <div data-role="footer" data-theme="b"><h2>Copyright</h2></div>
</div>
```

By default, the header of the collapsible content area includes the custom data-theme; but without the data-content-theme, the body of the collapsible content area remains the same theme as the containing content area. **Figure 11.7** shows an example of the collapsible content area with a custom data-theme and data-content-theme, so that both match.

FORM AND FORM ELEMENT THEMING

jQuery Mobile lets you create individual theme forms and form elements. Like everything else, forms and form elements inherit the swatch theme of the page component they're contained within. However, the data-theme can be used to customize the look and feel of an individual form, all forms, or certain form elements. Let's start by theming an entire form. The following code shows an example of a form that includes the "e" theme, while the page component includes the "b" theme. Notice that the form element also includes its own content data-role, otherwise the form would inherit the data-theme of the containing content area:

```
<div data-role="page" data-theme="b">
    <div data-role="header" data-theme="b">
        <h1>jQueryMobile.tv</h1>
        <a href="#" data-theme="e" data-icon="home">Home</a>
    </div>
    <div data-role="content" data-theme="d">
        <p>This content area includes the "d" swatch.</p>
        <form data-role="content" data-theme="e">
            <label for="my-text-input">My text input</label>
            <input type="text" name="name" id="my-text-input"
            ⇢ value="" />
            <a href="#" type="submit" data-role="button"
            ⇢ data-inline="true">Button</a>
        </form>
    </div>
    <div data-role="footer" data-theme="b"><h2>Copyright</h2></div>
</div>
```

FIGURE 11.8 A form that contains its own data-theme, separate from its containing content area.

It's useful to be able to assign different data-theme values to nested content areas. The form shows how these might be used to differentiate certain content (**Figure 11.8**).

To change the swatch on an individual form element, simply apply the data-theme to the actual element.

```
<a href="#" type="submit" data-role="button" data-inline="true"
➝ data-theme="b">Button</a>
```

This sets the button to a different theme from the rest of the form. In this case, it helps identify the button within the form, drawing attention to it visually (**Figure 11.9**).

LIST

Lists are probably the most complex component in jQuery Mobile, because they're the only element that includes additional attributes for theme options. For example, the listview can contain not only list items, but also dividers, count bubbles, and split buttons, all of which have their own theme options, as we'll see in this section. First, like the previous components discussed in this chapter, the listview itself can contain a data-theme, which will be inherited by any of its contained items:

FIGURE 11.9 Setting an individual form element's swatch value using the **data-theme** attribute.

```
<div data-role="page" data-theme="b">
    <div data-role="header" data-theme="b">
        <h1>jQueryMobile.tv</h1>
        <a href="#" data-theme="e" data-icon="home">Home</a>
    </div>
    <div data-role="content" data-theme="d">
        <p>This content area includes the "d" swatch.</p>
        <ul data-role="listview" data-inset="true" data-theme="e">
            <li><a href="#">List item</a></li>
            <li><a href="#">List item</a></li>
```

```
            <li><a href="#">List item</a></li>
            <li><a href="#">List item</a></li>
        </ul>
    </div>
    <div data-role="footer" data-theme="b"><h2>Copyright</h2></div>
</div>
```

Figure 11.10 shows an example of how this markup renders on a mobile device. As you can see, the list can have its own theme, separate from the rest of the page. However, if no data-theme is defined, the listview simply inherits the theme from the page or its content container.

It's also possible for individual list items to override the listview theme. If it makes sense for a specific list item to stand apart from the others, simply add a data-theme attribute to it:

```
<ul data-role="listview" data-inset="true" data-theme="e">
    <li>5</li>
    <li>20</li>
    <li>75</li>
    <li data-theme="a">Total = 100</li>
</ul>
```

Figure 11.11 shows an example of this listview that includes the "e" swatch as its data-theme and a list item that overrides that theme with the "a" swatch. In this particular case, this functionality is helpful, because it highlights and draws attention to a specific list item.

FIGURE 11.10 A listview with a custom theme.

FIGURE 11.11 A listview with a list item that has a different data-theme assigned to it.

FIGURE 11.12 A listview with
a list divider theme.

To theme dividers, there's a special attribute named data-divider-theme. This
attribute can be added to the listview to theme all list dividers:

```
<ul data-role="listview" data-inset="true" data-theme="e"
→ data-divider-theme="b">
    <li data-role="list-divider" role="heading">My number list</li>
    <li>5</li>
    <li>20</li>
    <li>75</li>
    <li data-theme="a">Total = 100</li>
</ul>
```

Figure 11.12 shows this code in action with the listview using the
data-divider-theme attribute for its dividers.

FIGURE 11.13 A listview with a count bubble theme.

Count bubbles can be themed with the data-count-theme attribute, which can be applied to the listview ul element to theme all count bubbles within the list:

```
<ul data-role="listview" data-inset="true" data-theme="e" data-
divider-theme="b" data-count-theme="b">

    <li data-role="list-divider" role="heading">My number list</li>

    <li>List item <span class="ui-li-count">5</span></li>

    <li>List item <span class="ui-li-count">20</span></li>

    <li>List item <span class="ui-li-count">75</span></li>

    <li data-theme="a">Total <span class="ui-li-count">100</span>
    </li>

</ul>
```

Figure 11.13 shows an example of the count bubble theme.

FIGURE 11.14 A listview with a data-split-theme.

Split buttons let you set two separate links in the same list item. To create a separate theme for these split buttons, you can add the data-split-theme attribute to the listview ul element:

```
<ul data-role="listview" data-inset="true" data-theme="e"
→ data-split=theme="b">
    <li>
        <a href="#link1">List item</a>
        <a href="#link1Alt">Split example</a>
    </li>
    <li>
        <a href="#link2">List item</a>
        <a href="#link2Alt">Split example</a>
    </li>
</ul>
```

Figure 11.14 shows an example of the data-split-theme.

WRAPPING **UP**

jQuery Mobile themes are easy to use and powerful at the same time. Every component can be themed, and when prebuilt swatches are not enough, you can always go custom. Between the ThemeRoller and the ability to manually edit existing classes, you should be well on your way to creating your own custom themes.

PART IV

THE
MOBILE API

12

GLOBAL OPTIONS

On the surface, the jQuery Mobile framework offers a quick and easy way to create mobile websites. However, the framework also has an application programming interface (API) that can be used to extend the basic functionality. The jQuery Mobile API provides an extra level of control over the customization of your mobile website. Everything from the custom setup of global options to hooking into interaction events and working with exposed methods is possible with the API. By the end of this chapter, you'll know how to define custom options for your mobile website and how to write custom code that interacts with the jQuery Mobile framework.

EXTENDING THE MOBILEINIT EVENT

As introduced earlier, jQuery Mobile includes an initialization event, named mobileinit, that loads before jQuery's document.ready event loads. This lets you override and extend jQuery Mobile's default global options, which is where all customization begins.

To extend the mobileinit event you need to order your JavaScript files correctly. Your custom JavaScript event handler must be included before jQuery Mobile is loaded and after the jQuery framework has loaded:

```
<script src="http://ajax.googleapis.com/ajax/libs/jquery/1.7.1/
→ jquery.min.js"></script>
<script src="assets/js/custom-jqm.js"></script>
<script src="http://code.jquery.com/mobile/1.0.1/
→ jquery.mobile-1.0.1.min.js"></script>
```

To extend the mobileinit event you must first bind an anonymous callback function to it, so you execute your custom code when the event fires:

```
$(document).bind("mobileinit", function() {
    // Override global options here
});
```

Once you've successfully bound a callback function to the `mobileinit` event, you can easily override the global options. The `$.mobile` object is the starting point for setting all properties. This is where you'll override global options that affect the way your mobile website functions. To override the global options, you can use jQuery's extend method to extend the `$.mobile` object:

```
$(document).bind("mobileinit", function() {
    $.extend( $.mobile, {
        property: value
    });
});
```

Or, you can simply override individual properties by setting them directly using the `$.mobile` object:

```
$(document).bind("mobileinit", function() {
    $.mobile.property = value;
    // Set other properties
});
```

If you want to update multiple properties, the extend method is a cleaner option because you don't need to write the `$.mobile` object multiple times. However, if you have only one property to update, setting the property individually requires less code.

CREATING CUSTOM **NAMESPACES**

The HTML5 data- attributes, such as `data-role`, can be customized through namespaces. A namespace lets you add a custom name that appears between the data- and -role portion of the `data-role` attribute, for example. This property can be useful for customizing your code. It can also prevent name collisions in the future as more third-party plug-ins are developed and possibly included in your project. The `$.mobile` property for customizing the namespace is `ns`:

```
$(document).bind("mobileinit", function() {
    $.mobile.ns = "jquerymobiletv-";
});
```

You can set the `ns` option to any custom value, such as `jquerymobiletv-`. Using the custom namespace produces:

```
data-jquerymobiletv-foo
```

Notice that a dash has been included at the end of the namespace; without it the result won't include a dash in your namespace, so your `data-` attributes will be hard to read and jQuery Mobile will look for an attribute that looks like this:

```
data-jquerymobiletvfoo
```

Be aware that choosing a custom namespace requires you to commit to that namespace while coding. During coding you'll include this custom namespace in your markup for any data- attributes that you use. Again, this not only customizes your markup, it can also prevent name collisions in the future if third-party plug-ins are used. Here's an example showing a custom `jquerymobiletv-` namespace:

```
<!DOCTYPE html>
<html>
<head>
    <meta http-equiv="Content-Type" content="text/html;
    → charset=UTF-8">
    <meta name="viewport" content="width=device-width,
    → initial-scale=1">
    <title>Custom Namespace - jQuery Mobile: Design and Develop
    → </title>
```

```
<link rel="stylesheet" href="http://code.jquery.com/
    mobile/1.0.1/jquery.mobile-1.0.1.min.css" />

<script src="http://ajax.googleapis.com/ajax/libs/jquery/1.7.1/
    jquery.min.js"></script>

<script src="http://code.jquery.com/mobile/1.0.1/
    jquery.mobile-1.0.1.min.js"></script>
</head>

<body>
    <div data-jquerymobiletv-role="page">
        <div data-jquerymobiletv-role="header"><h1>Page Name</h1>
            </div>
        <div data-jquerymobiletv-role="content"><p>Body Copy</p>
            </div>
        <div data-jquerymobiletv-role="footer">Copyright</div>
    </div>
</body>

</html>
```

The nice thing about using custom namespaces is that no other modifications are necessary; the code has the same results as running a jQuery Mobile webpage using the default namespaces.

It's even possible to use Cascading Style Sheets (CSS) selectors to choose certain HTML elements that include custom data- attributes. For example, you could select a jQuery Mobile page element and apply CSS to it:

```
.ui-mobile [data-jquerymobiletv-role="page"] {
    /* Custom CSS here */
}
```

With the introduction of data- attributes, developers have much more control over the data that is added to a webpage. Custom attributes provide a means for supporting semantic HTML, while enhancing the webpage with front-end scripting languages, such as JavaScript.

DELAYING PAGE INITIALIZATION

Page initialization happens automatically and by default with jQuery Mobile. The framework includes a property named autoInitializePage that determines whether the webpage should be initialized. By default, the value of this property is set to true, so the page is always initialized when the document is ready. However, by extending the $.mobile object it's possible to set this property to false and handle page initialization later.

You can temporarily delay page initialization while other scripts run, which is a perfect scenario for setting the autoInitializePage property to false:

```
$(document).bind("mobileinit", function() {

    $.extend( $.mobile , {

        autoInitializePage: false

    });

});
```

Imagine a large amount of client-side JavaScript having to be loaded, such as a long list of names. In cases like this it might be a good idea to delay initialization until the document object model (DOM) has completed loading. This way the client-side JavaScript has a chance to run and you can fade the data in gracefully rather than having it load line by line before the visitor's eyes:

```
<!DOCTYPE html>

<html>

<head>

    <meta http-equiv="Content-Type" content="text/html;
    → charset=UTF-8">

    <meta name="viewport" content="width=device-width,
    → initial-scale=1">

    <title>Page Initialization - jQuery Mobile: Design and Develop
    → </title>

    <link rel="stylesheet" href="http://code.jquery.com/
    → mobile/1.0.1/jquery.mobile-1.0.1.min.css" />
```

```
<script src="http://ajax.googleapis.com/ajax/libs/jquery/1.7.1/
  → jquery.min.js"></script>
<script src="assets/js/custom-jqm.js"></script>
<script src="http://code.jquery.com/mobile/1.0.1/
  → jquery.mobile-1.0.1.min.js"></script>
</head>
<body>
    <div data-jquerymobiletv-role="page" id="mypage">
        <div data-jquerymobiletv-role="header"><h1>Page Name</h1>
          → </div>
        <div data-jquerymobiletv-role="content">
            <ul data-jquerymobiletv-role="listview" id="my-list">
              → </ul>
        </div>
        <div data-jquerymobiletv-role="footer">Copyright</div>
    </div>
    <script type="text/javascript">
        $("#mypage").css('display', 'none');
        var namesArray = new Array("Tom", "Lucy", "Lee", "Chris",
          → "Albert", "Frank");
        for(var i=0; i<namesArray.length; i++) {
            $('#my-list').append('<li><a href="#">'+namesArray[i]+
              → '</a></li>');
        }
        $.mobile.autoInitializePage = true;
        $("#mypage").fadeIn(1000);
    </script>
</body>
</html>
```

FIGURE 12.1 A page rendered after delaying page initialization.

Running this code delays initialization; the user won't see the list of names until the loop has completed and the autoInitializePage property is set to true, then the jQuery fadeIn method is used to fade in the page.

Figure 12.1 shows how the page renders once the autoInitializePage property is set to true and the page is faded in.

CUSTOMIZING THE subPageUrlKey

The subPageUrlKey is a URL query string parameter that's used as a reference for subpages generated by jQuery Mobile widgets, which were covered earlier in the book. This URL parameter has a key of ui-page by default. However, this key can be changed through the subPageUrlKey property, which is a property of the $.mobile object. A string value can be used to update the value of this property, which will reflect in widget-generated subpage URLs.

Creating a custom subPageUrlKey not only creates more attractive URLs, but also may shorten URLs or set their values to something more specific to the website that's using them.

For example, if a custom subPageUrlKey of jqmtv-page used a default URL of:

```
web-page.html&ui-page=value
```

it would become:

```
web-page.html&jqmtv-page=value
```

USING **ACTIVE PAGE** AND **BUTTON CLASSES**

Webpages that include the jQuery Mobile framework have a default CSS class that's automatically applied to the page element named ui-page-active. But you can change this default behavior by changing or appending to the default value of the active page class. The $.mobile object has a property named activePageClass that can be modified. If this class is replaced with a new value, the default CSS included with the framework no longer applies its styling to the ui-page-active class since it no longer exists. Therefore it's important to create your own custom CSS class that corresponds to the value you provide for this property or append an additional class to the ui-page-active class:

```
$(document).bind("mobileinit", function() {
    $.extend( $.mobile, {
        activePageClass: "ui-page-active ui-jqmtv-page-active"
    });
});
```

By appending an additional custom class, the existing CSS is left intact and the focus shifts to the CSS that's used for customizations, rather than every minute design detail of the framework. A simple CSS file needs to be created and included to apply some styles to the new custom CSS class:

```
.ui-jqmtv-page-active {
    background: #09C;
    color: #fff;
    text-shadow: none;
}
```

This CSS applies a new background color or text color and removes the text shadowing from the webpage when included in the HTML markup. Here's an example of a simple HTML file that includes the CSS and the custom activePageClass setting from the previous examples:

```
<!DOCTYPE html>
<html>
<head>
    <meta http-equiv="Content-Type" content="text/html;
    → charset=UTF-8">
    <meta name="viewport" content="width=device-width,
    → initial-scale=1">
    <title>Active Page Class - jQuery Mobile: Design and Develop
    → </title>
    <link rel="stylesheet" href="http://code.jquery.com/
    → mobile/1.0.1/jquery.mobile-1.0.1.min.css" />
    <link rel="stylesheet" href="assets/css/jqmtv.css" />
    <script src="http://ajax.googleapis.com/ajax/libs/jquery/1.7.1/
    → jquery.min.js"></script>
    <script src="assets/js/custom-jqm-apc.js"></script>
    <link rel="stylesheet" hr<script src="http://code.jquery.com/
    → mobile/1.0.1/jquery.mobile-1.0.1.min.js"></script>
</head>
<body>
    <div data-role="page">
        <div data-role="header"><h1>Page Name</h1></div>
        <div data-role="content">
            <p>Body copy</p>
        </div>
        <div data-role="footer">Copyright</div>
    </div>
</body>
</html>
```

FIGURE 12.2 A custom active
page class inserted by the
framework based on the global
configuration settings.

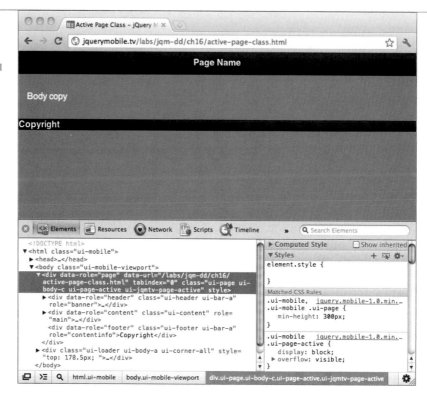

With the jQuery Mobile framework added, this code is transformed to include
many additional classes and attributes. The custom `ui-jqmtv-page-active` class
can be seen in the markup when using any type of browser development tools.

Figure 12.2 shows how the markup is transformed by the framework to include
the new class we created and applied the CSS to.

Another property named `activeBtnClass` works exactly the same as the
`activePageClass`. You can set it in the `mobileinit` callback. It can contain any
string value, and the string value can ultimately relate to a custom CSS class that
you can include in a CSS file. The only difference in the `activePageClass` and the
`activeBtnClass` properties is that the `activeBtnClass` lets you style the active
state of any buttons that are used.

ENABLING AND DISABLING
AJAX NAVIGATION

By default, Ajax-based navigation is set to true using the $.mobile object's ajaxEnabled property. However, this property can be set to false in a configuration file:

```
$(document).bind("mobileinit", function() {
    $.extend( $.mobile, {
        ajaxEnabled: false
    });
});
```

This is such a simple property to modify, but it has major results. Setting this property to false disables URL hash listening and loads all URLs as standard HTTP requests. Doing so causes page refreshes, disables page preloading and caching, and eliminates page and dialog transitions. If you'd like your mobile website to function as a standard website, setting this option to false will create standard HTTP requests.

ALTERING THE DEFAULT PAGE AND DIALOG TRANSITIONS

By default, pages and dialogs include a transition effect in jQuery Mobile when page changes are handled via Ajax. The default page transition is slide, while the default dialog transition is pop. To change these values, target the defaultPageTransition and/or the defaultDialogTransition properties:

```
$(document).bind("mobileinit", function() {
    $.extend( $.mobile , {
        defaultPageTransition: "fade",
        defaultDialogTransition: "fade"
    });
});
```

If you run this code, you'll see that the transitions for pages and dialogs will both be a fade:

```
<!DOCTYPE html>
<html>
<head>
    <meta http-equiv="Content-Type" content="text/html;
    → charset=UTF-8">
    <meta name="viewport" content="width=device-width,
    → initial-scale=1">
    <title>Page Transitions - jQuery Mobile: Design and Develop
    → </title>
    <link rel="stylesheet" href="http://code.jquery.com/mobile/
    → 1.0.1/jquery.mobile-1.0.1.min.css" />
    <script src="http://ajax.googleapis.com/ajax/libs/jquery/1.7.1/
    → jquery.min.js"></script>
    <script src="assets/js/custom-jqm-transitions.js"></script>
    <script src="http://code.jquery.com/mobile/1.0.1/
    → jquery.mobile-1.0.1.min.js"></script>
</head>
```

```
<body>
    <div data-role="page">
        <div data-role="header"><h1>Page Name</h1></div>
        <div data-role="content">
            <p><a href="sample-page.html">Open Another Page</a></p>
            <p><a href="dialog.html" data-rel="dialog">Open Dialog
               ⤷ </a></p>
        </div>
        <div data-role="footer">Copyright</div>
    </div>
</body>
</html>
```

The framework includes six CSS-based transition effects: slide, slideup, slidedown, pop, fade, flip, which were all covered in detail in Chapter 4, "Creating Multipage Websites with jQuery Mobile." These effects can also be applied directly on hyperlinks by including the data-transition attribute:

```
<a href="sample-page.html" data-transition="flip">Data transition</a>
```

Using this code overrides any previous settings for transitions.

WRAPPING **UP**

The jQuery Mobile framework is simple to use, but don't let its simplicity fool you—there's a lot happening behind the curtain. There are many ways to add custom functionality to create powerful mobile websites and applications. Accessing the API allows fine-grained control that lets you tell the framework how to behave by default and even tie into every interaction that occurs on the client side through events. In the next chapter, you'll see how events can provide even more control over your custom jQuery Mobile project.

13

HOOKING
INTO EVENTS

jQuery Mobile offers custom events you can use to extend the functionality of the framework, including touch, scroll, device orientation, page transition, and page initialization, among others. Hooking into jQuery Mobile events opens up an entire world of opportunity that can't be achieved with the basic framework setup. Knowing the state of a webpage at any given time provides a level of control you can use to extend existing functionality. This chapter shows you how to hook into each of these events to create custom functionality in a mobile website.

TOUCH EVENTS

There are many touch events you can hook into with jQuery Mobile. Keep in mind that these are available only to touch-enabled devices, so desktop users may not experience them or any customizations added via an event hook. With that said, touch events won't cause errors on desktop devices: they simply won't function, because mouse events rule the desktop experience. These events can trigger a callback function that includes any custom JavaScript. **Table 13.1** describes the five different touch events accessible through the jQuery Mobile API.

Table 13.2 describes the swipe event properties mentioned in Table 13.1.

TABLE 13.1 Touch events

EVENT	DESCRIPTION
tap	Responds to a quick tap and removal of a finger from the device screen.
taphold	Responds to a tap of a finger that is left in place on the device screen for about one second.
swipe	Responds when a webpage is dragged horizontally or vertically. This is the only event that has associated properties. These properties are listed in Table 13.2.
swipeleft	Responds when the webpage is dragged to the left.
swiperight	Responds when the webpage is dragged to the right.

TABLE 13.2 swipe event properties

EVENT	DESCRIPTION
scrollSupressionThreshold	The default value is 10 pixels. If the value is greater than this, then scrolling is suppressed.
durationThreshold	The default value is 1000 milliseconds. If the interaction is longer than this, then it's no longer considered a swipe and nothing occurs.
horizontalDistanceThreshold	The default value is 30 pixels. The horizontal displacement of the swipe must be greater than this.
verticalDistanceThreshold	The default value is 75 pixels. The vertical displacement of the swipe must be less than this.

To bind to any of these touch events, you must use the `document.ready` event. Once the document is ready, you can access an HTML element and bind your selected touch event:

```
$(document).ready(function(){
    $(".test-tap-hold").bind("taphold", function(event) {
        $(this).html("Tapped and held");
    });
});
```

Once the document is ready, the taphold event is bound to an element with the class name `.test-tap-hold`. When a finger touches this element and remains on it, the taphold event is fired. The following example incorporates the JavaScript file that binds this event to the HTML element:

```
<!DOCTYPE HTML>
<html>
<head>
    <meta http-equiv="Content-Type" content="text/html;
    → charset=UTF-8">
    <meta name="viewport" content="width=device-width,
    → initial-scale=1">
    <title>taphold- jQuery Mobile: Design and Develop</title>
    <link rel="stylesheet" href="http://code.jquery.com/
    → mobile/1.0.1/jquery.mobile-1.0.1.min.css" />
    <script src="http://ajax.googleapis.com/ajax/libs/jquery/1.7.1/
    → jquery.min.js"></script>
    <script src="http://code.jquery.com/mobile/1.0.1/
    → jquery.mobile-1.0.1.min.js"></script>
</head>
<body>
    <div data-role="page">
        <div data-role="header">
```

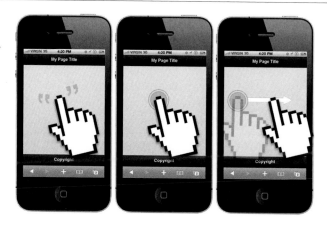

```
        <h1>Page title</h1>
    </div>
    <div data-role="content">
        <ul data-role="listview">
            <li class="test-tap-hold">Tap and hold test</li>
        </ul>
    </div>
    <div data-role="footer">
        Copyright
    </div>
    </div>
</body>
</html>
```

As you can see, a listview is included in the page with a list item that contains a class name of test-tap-hold. When this element is touched and the user's finger remains in this position on the screen, the event is fired and the HTML value gets updated. **Figure 13.1** illustrates examples of different touch events.

The events in Table 13.1 let you tie custom code into any state of a mobile website. Knowing when and how a user is interacting with the screen gives you a foundation for responding to those interactions.

ORIENTATION EVENTS

FIGURE 13.2 Webpages can display vertically or horizontally depending on the orientation of the device.

The jQuery Mobile framework includes a single orientation event named orientationchange. This event is fired any time the device is rotated vertically or horizontally (**Figure 13.2**).

The orientation of the device can be determined during rotation by accessing the orientation property within the orientationchange event. This property returns a read-only value of either portrait or landscape. To hook into the orientationchange event, the body element must be bound to the event:

```
$(document).ready(function(){

    $('body').bind('orientationchange', function(event) {

        console.log('orientationchange: '+ event.orientation);

    });

});
```

Of course, it's also important to bind the event after the document is ready so the body is accessible, otherwise you'll receive inconsistent results. You can also take this code a step further by using the jQuery trigger method to manually trigger the orientationchange event when the document is ready:

```
$(document).ready(function(){

    $('body').bind('orientationchange', function(event) {

        console.log('orientationchange: '+ event.orientation);
```

```
    });
    $('body').trigger('orientationchange');
});
```

Triggering the event manually when the document is ready makes it possible to determine the orientation automatically when the page first loads, which otherwise would not occur. The orientation values are also added to the <html> element within the webpage and are therefore accessible through CSS. This provides a way to respond to a device's orientation via jQuery Mobile and CSS through what is called responsive design.

RESPONSIVE DESIGN

With the plethora of devices available on the market today, it's becoming more and more important to design websites that display properly in all the different formats. Responsive design is just that: displaying content based on the device format. This includes device size, device orientation, and even the way your site reacts to browser resizing on desktop machines. Common ways of achieving responsive design are through CSS media queries or simply serving an alternative website. jQuery Mobile provides a solution that responds automatically.

In other words, knowing the device's orientation at any given time helps you determine how to render the layout of your content. With this sort of power it's not necessary to have multiple websites to handle different devices.

SCROLL EVENTS

jQuery Mobile offers two scroll events that are triggered when a user scrolls a webpage: scrollstart and scrollstop. The scrollstart event triggers when a page scroll begins. Like the orientationchange event, the scrollstart event must be bound to the body element when the document is ready:

```
$(document).ready(function(){
    $('body').bind('scrollstart', function(event) {
        console.log("scrollstart");
    });
});
```

The scrollstop event fires when the page scroll stops. Binding the scrollstop event to the body element works the same way as binding the scrollstart event:

```
$(document).ready(function(){
    $('body').bind('scrollstart', function(event) {
        console.log("scrollstart");
    });
    $('body').bind('scrollstop', function(event) {
        console.log("scrollstop");
    });
});
```

Scroll events can be used together to run custom JavaScript. For example, they can be used to create a lazy loading effect, functionality that loads images on demand as they are revealed lower on the webpage during scrolling:

```
$(document).ready(function() {
    var _scrollInterval;
    $(document).bind({
        scrollstart: function() {
            _scrollInterval = setInterval("onScroll()", 50);
        },
```

```
                    scrollstop: function() {
                        clearInterval(_scrollInterval);
                    }
                });
            });
            function onScroll() {
                lazyLoad();
            };
            function lazyLoad() {
                $('img').each(function(index){
                    var viewableWindowPosition = $(window).scrollTop() +
                    →  $(window).height();
                    var viewableImagePosition = $(this).position().top +
                    →  $(this).height();
                    if($(this).hasClass('lazy-img') && viewableWindowPosition >=
                    →  viewableImagePosition && $(this).attr('data-image')) {
                        $(this).attr('src', $(this).attr('data-image'));
                        $(this).attr('data-image', '');
                        $(this).css('display', 'none');
                        $(this).fadeIn(1000, function() {
                            // Image faded in
                        });
                    }
                });
            }
```

The images are not rendered initially, but as the webpage is scrolled, the images load when the area of the page they are in is revealed. This functionality produces a quicker page load time because all the images load the same loader image by default, rather than loading each unique image until scrolling reveals them on the screen.

This example expects image tags that are loaded lazily to include a `data-image` attribute and a class with a value of `lazy-img`:

```
<img src="assets/img/loading.gif" data-image="assets/img/
  trademark-jquerymobiletv.png" class="lazy-img">
```

The `lazy-img` class is used to determine which images to load lazily, and the `data-image` attribute is used as a reference to the unique image for that tag that is loaded when the portion of the page is revealed in the browser. There are endless possibilities for adding custom functionality using the scroll events; this is just one example, but it is a powerful one that increases the speed at which webpages load.

FIGURE 13.3 The four events associated with jQuery Mobile's page transition process.

Imagine knowing when a page transition is going to occur before it even happens. Add to that knowing ahead of time when a page is going to hide. With page transition events, this is possible. jQuery Mobile page animations are powered by page transitions. The animations used during the transition between pages were defined in previous chapters, but there are also events associated with each step of a page transition. Events occur before and after each page transition and can be used to execute custom code at any time during this process. As shown in **Figure 13.3**, four events are associated with page transitions, and they occur in sequence.

The first two events occur on the page currently in view when the page transition begins, and the final two events occur on the page that is coming into view.

Attaching event handlers to these events is easy with the jQuery on method. You can attach an event handler to a single element for each of the events. In the following example, the on method is attached to div#my-page and allows custom event handlers to be created for each of the page transition events. The div with an id of my-page is being used as the page container in the HTML document, therefore at any step of page transition these events trigger the custom script that writes to the console:

```
$(document).ready(function() {
    $('div#my-page').on({
        pagebeforeshow: function(event, ui) {
            console.log('This page is about to be shown: '+
            → ui.prevPage);
        },
        pageshow: function(event, ui) {
            console.log('This page was just hidden: '+ ui.prevPage);
        },
        pagebeforehide: function(event, ui) {
            console.log('This page is about to be hidden: '+
            → ui.nextPage);
        },
```

```
      pagehide: function(event, ui) {
          console.log('This page was just shown: '+ ui.nextPage);
      }
  });
});
```

As you can see, each event also has event and ui parameters. The event parameter is the event object itself, while the ui parameter is a data object that includes a property that represents a page. Each event's ui object has a different associated page property:

- The pagebeforeshow event includes the prevPage property in its ui data object. This property represents the page that is about to be shown.

- The pagebeforehide event includes the nextPage property in its ui data object. This property represents the page that is being transitioned to.

- The pageshow event includes the prevPage property in its ui data object. This property represents the page that is being transitioned away from.

- The pagehide event includes the nextPage property in its ui data object. This property represents the page that is being transitioned to.

jQuery Mobile documentation uses the live method to attach handlers for page transition events; however, this method was deprecated in jQuery 1.7, and the delegate method is now being recommended for sites using older versions of jQuery. Setting up the delegate method is similar to using the on method:

```
$(document).ready(function() {
    $(document).delegate('div#my-page', {
        pagebeforeshow: function(event, ui) {
            console.log('This page is about to be shown: '+
            → ui.prevPage);
        },
        pageshow: function(event, ui) {
            console.log('This page was just hidden: '+ ui.prevPage);
        },
```

```
        pagebeforehide: function(event, ui) {
            console.log('This page is about to be hidden: '+
            →  ui.nextPage);
        },
        pagehide: function(event, ui) {
            console.log('This page was just shown: '+ ui.nextPage);
        }
    });
});
```

Being able to hook into page transition events gives you a lot of control. You can trigger custom code during any step in the page transition process. Knowing what page will be revealed before it happens gives you access to that page's HTML structure, which is useful for discarding unwanted markup, injecting additional markup into the page, and so on. This also holds true for pages that are about to become hidden: these events can be used to display a dialog or pop-up window, carry JavaScript properties from one page to another, and so on. The following script shows an example of a JavaScript property being carried from one page to another using these events:

```
$(document).ready(function() {
    $('div#my-page').on({
        pagebeforeshow: function(event, ui) {
            console.log('This page is about to be shown: '+
            →  ui.prevPage);
            thePreviousPage = ui.prevPage;
        },
        pageshow: function(event, ui) {
            console.log('This page was just hidden: '+ ui.prevPage);
        },
```

```
pagebeforehide: function(event, ui) {
    console.log('This page is about to be hidden: '+
    →  ui.nextPage);
    console.log('thePreviousPage: '+ thePreviousPage);
},
pagehide: function(event, ui) {
    console.log('This page was just shown: '+ ui.nextPage);
    console.log('thePreviousPage: '+ thePreviousPage);
}
});
});
```

As you can see, this sort of functionality can be very powerful, yet it's quite easy to achieve. Page transition events let you leverage page data at any point during the jQuery Mobile page life cycle.

PAGE **INITIALIZATION** AND
CUSTOM WIDGET CREATION

FIGURE 13.4 The three steps in jQuery Mobile's page initialization process.

The jQuery Mobile framework enhances basic HTML markup. This markup enhancement magic takes place when page initialization occurs. There are three steps to the page initialization process; they occur in the sequence defined in **Figure 13.4**.

The pagecreatebefore event occurs when the page is inserted into the DOM, before jQuery Mobile initializes plug-ins and enhances the webpage. The pagecreatebefore event presents a great opportunity to add markup to a webpage before the jQuery Mobile framework gets ahold of it and makes enhancements:

```
$('div#my-page').on('pagebeforecreate', function(event) {
    console.log('This page is about to be created');
    $('div#my-page').attr('data-title', 'My Page');
});
```

In the example above, a data-title was added to div#my-page before the jQuery Mobile framework enhanced the markup, therefore the data-title was used during the enhancement.

The pagecreate event occurs after the pagecreatebefore event and, therefore, after the page is created in the DOM. However, this event still takes place before the HTML markup is enhanced by the jQuery Mobile framework. The pagecreate event is the perfect place to create custom widgets. The following script creates a widget named logo, which has image, width, and height options:

```
(function($){
    $.widget("mobile.logo", $.mobile.widget, {
        // data-attributes that can be used in HTML markup (includes
        →  default values)
        options: {
            image: '',
            width: 200,
            height: 200
        },
```

```
// This method is required and called by jQuery Mobile to
→  initialize the method
_create: function() {
    console.log("Widget has been created");
    $(document).trigger("logocreate");
    var logoEl = this.element;
    logoEl.css('background',
    →  'url('+logoEl.attr('data-image')+')');
    logoEl.width(logoEl.attr('data-width'));
    logoEl.height(logoEl.attr('data-height'));
}
});
// The pagecreate event is used to initialize widget instances
$(document).bind("pagecreate", function(e) {
    $(document).trigger("logobeforecreate");
    return $(":jqmData(role='logo')", e.target).logo();
});
})(jQuery);
```

When the markup for the logo widget is included in the HTML document, the jQuery Mobile framework makes the enhancements according to the script in the _create method. The following markup shows how this widget would be included in a jQuery Mobile webpage:

```
<div data-role="logo" data-image="assets/img/trademark-
→  jquerymobiletv.png" data-width="200" data-height="30"></div>
```

The pagecreate event is bound to the document, so that when the page is created the framework finds the logo widget markup by its role using the :jqmData selector and then triggers the _create method. In this example, the widget's _create method accesses the data-attributes used in the markup to render the widget accordingly.

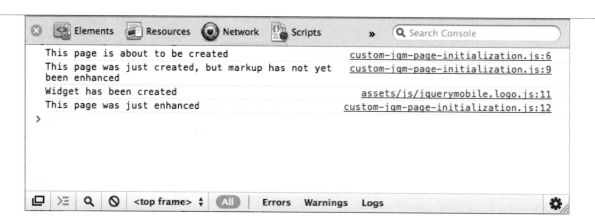

FIGURE 13.5 An example of each page initialization event as it is logged in Chrome.

The framework also includes a pageinit method, the final step of the page initialization process. This event is triggered after the page has been enhanced by the framework, which includes all existing and custom widget enhancements:

```
$('div#my-page').on('pageinit', function(event) {
    console.log('This page was just enhanced');
});
```

Figure 13.5 shows an example log in Chrome when running a webpage that includes the initialization and custom widget creation.

WRAPPING **UP**

Hooking into jQuery Mobile events opens up a world of opportunity. When you understand how to hook into jQuery Mobile events, you can create virtually any custom functionality you can imagine. From touch events to device orientation to page changes and transitions, all events are derived from the user. Knowing when and how to react to them is priceless.

14

WORKING WITH EXPOSED METHODS

The jQuery Mobile framework includes numerous methods and properties that have been exposed on the $.mobile object. Exposing a method means giving third-party access to it. In other words, jQuery Mobile offers third-party developers access to some of the internal methods used throughout its framework. These methods and properties let you tap into some core jQuery Mobile functionality to create customizations that set your mobile application apart from the rest. This chapter covers changing pages, preloading pages, and a number of utility methods and properties.

CHANGING PAGES PROGRAMMATICALLY

Changing pages programmatically means you can use code to direct the browser to another page with or without user interaction. One of several exposed methods in the jQuery Mobile framework is changePage, which adds functionality to standard hyperlinks and form submissions by providing a way to change pages programmatically. The equivalent to this method in basic JavaScript is document.location, which is sometimes used to achieve programmatic page changes. In addition to basic page changes, the typical jQuery Mobile visuals that occur, such as page loading and page transitions, are also available when you change pages programmatically via the framework's API. The changePage method is useful when content is dynamically added to the page. Let's add a click event to the logo widget that was created in Chapter 13, "Hooking into Events," so you can use changePage to change pages programmatically:

```
(function($){
    $.widget("mobile.logo", $.mobile.widget, {
        options: {
            image: '',
            width: 0,
            height: 0,
            hyperlink: '#'
        },
        _create: function() {
            $(document).trigger("logocreate");
            var logoEl = this.element;
            logoEl.css('background', 'url('+this.options.image+')');
            logoEl.width(this.options.width);
            logoEl.height(this.options.height);
```

```
    // This method will trigger a page change through the
 →  jQuery Mobile API
    logoEl.click(function() {
        console.log("Widget has been clicked: "+ $(this).
         →  attr('data-hyperlink'));
        $.mobile.changePage($(this).attr('data-hyperlink'));
    });
 }
});
$(document).bind("pagecreate", function(e) {
    $(document).trigger("logobeforecreate");
    return $(":jqmData(role='logo')", e.target).logo();
});
})(jQuery);
```

With the changePage method in place, the widget can change pages when a user selects it. In this example, the hyperlink is expected to be an HTML attribute, because the widget has an additional property that supports this option. With this option, each instance of the widget can include its own custom hyperlink in a data-hyperlink attribute:

```
<div data-role="logo" data-image="assets/img/trademark-
 →  jquerymobiletv.png" data-width="200" data-height="30"
 →  data-hyperlink="http://www.jquerymobile.tv"></div>
```

Although this may not be the most practical example, it shows how you can create a custom widget to handle any functionality. The changePage method requires at least one argument named to, which specifies the page to change during the request. The value of the to argument can be a string, as in this example, or a jQuery collection object. changePage also has other optional arguments that customize a request. **Table 14.1** lists the properties that can be added.

TABLE 14.1 The changePage properties

PROPERTIES	DESCRIPTIONS
allowSamePageTransition	When set to false (the default setting), will not execute a request to the same page. When set to true, allows the same page to be used as the to argument and executes it. (You might use this property for a form submission that sends form values and processes them on the same page.)
changeHash	Specifies whether or not the hash in the browser's location bar should be updated. The default value is true. A hash is a # sign in a URL.
data	Sends data with an Ajax request.
dataUrl	Value undefined by default, but can be set as a URL to update the browser location when the page changes.
pageContainer	Specifies what element the requested page will be contained in.
reloadPage	Forces the page to reload if a URL is used as the value for the changePage method.
reverse	Changes the direction of a page transition.
showLoadMsg	Specifies whether or not to show a loading message.
role	Defines the data-role associated with the page when it is displayed.
transition	Specifies the transition used when changing pages.
type	Sets the type of request to post or get. The default value is get.

Adding a property to the options argument is as simple as making a comma-delimited list of the properties using JavaScript Object Notation (JSON) and setting the specific individual values.

NOTE: JSON is a lightweight JavaScript data format that can be used to exchange data between systems or a webpage and a database. jQuery uses JSON throughout its libraries to pass data and set values.

These optional arguments can provide complex functionality. For example, you can set a request type to submit form values:

```
$(document).ready(function() {
    $('#next-btn').click(function() {
        $.mobile.changePage( "step2.php", {
            type: "post",
            data: $("form#my-form").serialize()
        });
    });

});
```

This might be helpful in a multistep process where form values are carried from one page to another. The following example includes a form with an input field for an email address. Rather than a submit button, this form includes an anchor element with an id of next-btn, which when clicked, triggers the changePage method in the previous example:

```
<!DOCTYPE HTML>
<html>
<head>
    <meta http-equiv="Content-Type" content="text/html;
    → charset=UTF-8">
```

```
<meta name="viewport" content="width=device-width,
  initial-scale=1">

<title>changePage Form Submission - jQuery Mobile: Design and
  Develop</title>

<link rel="stylesheet" href="http://code.jquery.com/
  mobile/1.0.1/jquery.mobile-1.0.1.min.css" />

<script src="http://ajax.googleapis.com/ajax/libs/jquery/1.7.1/
  jquery.min.js"></script>

<script src="http://code.jquery.com/mobile/1.0.1/
  jquery.mobile-1.0.1.min.js"></script>

<script src="assets/js/custom-jqm-changepage-formsubmission.js">
  </script>
</head>
<body>
    <div data-role="page">
        <div data-role="header"><h1>Page Header</h1></div>
        <div data-role="content">
            <form action="" id="my-form">
                <label for="emailAddress">Email Address</label>
                <input type="text" name="emailAddress"
                  id="emailAddress">
            </form>
            <a href="#" id="next-btn">Next</a>
        </div>
        <div data-role="footer">Copyright</div>
    </div>
</body>
</html>
```

The changePage method is set to change to a page named step2.php, with the type property set as a post request and the data property set as the forms serialized data. The form includes a single input named emailAddress; when the page changes, the value of the emailAddress input is sent to step2.php:

```
<!DOCTYPE HTML>
<html>
<head>
    <meta http-equiv="Content-Type" content="text/html;
    → charset=UTF-8">
    <meta name="viewport" content="width=device-width,
    → initial-scale=1">
    <title>changePage Form Submission: Step 2 - jQuery Mobile:
    → Design and Develop</title>
</head>
<body>
    <div data-role="page">
        <div data-role="header"><h1>Page Header</h1></div>
        <div data-role="content">
            <form action="">
                <label for="firstName">First Name:</label>
                <input type="text" name="firstName" id="firstName">
                <label for="lastName">Last Name:</label>
                <input type="text" name="lastName" id="lastName">
                <label for="emailAddress">Email Address</label>
                <input type="text" name="emailAddress"
                → id="emailAddress" value="<?php echo
                → $_POST['emailAddress']; ?>">
                <input type="submit" value="Sign me up">
            </form>
```

```
            </div>
            <div data-role="footer">Copyright</div>
        </div>
    </body>
</html>
```

The `step2.php` page includes additional form input fields to get more information from the user before he officially submits the form. This example could be used as a sign-up form for a newsletter, for example, gathering an email address and then asking for a first and last name before actually submitting the form. The `emailAddress` is carried over from the previous page through PHP's `$_POST` array and written to the corresponding field.

The `changePage` method is a powerful means to handle not only page changes, but also form submissions. It allows you to customize page changes in many interesting and unique ways.

LOADING PAGES SILENTLY

Another great $.mobile object method is loadPage. You can use the loadPage method to load external pages without displaying them. This is a useful way to preload pages so they display quicker when the user clicks a link. To use this method, you need to write code much like we did for the changePage method. First, of course, you have to wait for the document to be ready or the page to be created. Then, when either of those events triggers, you can call the loadPage event to preload one or multiple pages:

```
$(document).ready(function() {
    $.mobile.loadPage("page2.html");
});
```

This method is so incredibly easy to use and offers huge benefits. The following example embeds a JavaScript file that includes the loadPage code:

```
<!DOCTYPE HTML>
<html>
<head>
    <meta http-equiv="Content-Type" content="text/html;
    → charset=UTF-8">
    <meta name="viewport" content="width=device-width,
    → initial-scale=1">
    <title>loadPage- jQuery Mobile: Design and Develop</title>
    <link rel="stylesheet" href="http://code.jquery.com/
    → mobile/1.0.1/jquery.mobile-1.0.1.min.css" />
    <script src="http://ajax.googleapis.com/ajax/libs/jquery/1.7.1/
    → jquery.min.js"></script>
    <script src="http://code.jquery.com/mobile/1.0.1/
    → jquery.mobile-1.0.1.min.js"></script>
    <script src="assets/js/custom-jqm-loadpage.js"></script>
</head>
<body>
```

```
<div data-role="page">
    <div data-role="header"><h1>Page Header</h1></div>
    <div data-role="content">
        <a href="page2.html">Link to another page</a>
    </div>
    <div data-role="footer">Copyright</div>
</div>
</body>
</html>
```

As soon as the page is loaded and the document is ready, the page2.html file loads silently in the background before any link is clicked. When the user clicks the anchor element that links to the page2.html page, the file displays immediately. **Figure 14.1** shows an example of the markup after the page has been loaded via the loadPage method. As you can see, the page has been loaded and inserted into the bottom of the current page.

The loadPage method includes a required url argument that can be a string representing a relative or absolute URL or it can be an object. **Table 14.2** lists the properties available in a loadPage request.

TABLE 14.2 The loadPage properties

PROPERTIES	DESCRIPTIONS
data	Sends data to the page being loaded, similar to the data property in the changePage method.
loadMsgDelay	Specifies a delay in milliseconds to allow time to fetch the loading page before showing the message.
pageContainer	Specifies the element that will contain the page after it has been loaded.
reloadPage	Forces a page refresh.
role	Specifies a data-role on the loaded page once it is displayed.
type	Specifies the request to load the page as a post or get.

FIGURE 14.1 An example of the markup after the `loadPage` method has loaded the `page2.html` example. As you can see, the page is loaded, but not currently displayed.

WORKING WITH UTILITY METHODS

jQuery Mobile has several built-in utility methods that provide useful functionality when developing a website. **Table 14.3** lists the current utility methods supported by the framework and a description of what each of them does.

TABLE 14.3 Utility methods

METHODS	DESCRIPTIONS
jqmData	Provides a way to add data to any DOM element.
jqmRemoveData	Provides a way to remove data from any DOM element.
$.mobile.showPageLoadingMsg	Shows the loading message, which can be done at any point in time. Useful when dynamically modifying the page.
$.mobile.hidePageLoadingMsg	Hides the loading message at any time.
$.mobile.fixedToolbars.show	Displays fixed headers and footers of the active page. A single, optional, Boolean argument named immediately can be set to true to immediately show the header or footer. By default this argument is false, which fades in the header and footer after 100 milliseconds.
$.mobile.fixedToolbars.hide	Hides fixed headers and footers of the active page. Includes a single, optional argument named immediately, as in the $.mobile.fixedToolbars.show method.
$.mobile.path.parseUrl	Parses a URL into an object. The resulting object includes 16 properties, which are listed in Table 14.4.
$.mobile.path.makePathAbsolute	Converts a relative path to an absolute path.
$.mobile.path.makeUrlAbsolute	Converts a relative URL to an absolute URL.
$.mobile.path.isSameDomain	Compares two URLs.
$.mobile.path.isRelativeUrl	Determines whether or not a URL is relative.
$.mobile.path.isAbsoluteUrl	Determines whether or not a URL is absolute.
$.mobile.base	Works with the generated base element. jQuery Mobile generates a base element in the head of the HTML file that is updated automatically when a new page is loaded. This element keeps a reference to the currently loaded page so all assets are loaded from the proper location.
$.mobile.silentScroll	Accepts one argument that can be used to scroll a page to a specific Y position. Does not trigger the scroll event listeners.

In addition to the mentioned utility methods, there is the `$.mobile.activePage` property, which is used as a reference to the current page in view.

Table 14.4 lists the properties associated with the object that's returned from the `$.mobile.path.parseUrl` method call. Each of these properties represents a component of the URL and is expressed as a string.

TABLE 14.4 `$.mobile.path.parseUrl` properties

PROPERTIES	DESCRIPTIONS
hash	Represents the portion of the URL that comes directly after the # and includes the # character.
host	Represents the host and port of the URL.
hostname	Represents the name of the host of the URL.
href	Represents the complete URL.
pathname	Represents any path or directory and the current file referenced in the URL.
port	If specified, represents the port within the URL.
protocol	Represents the protocol of the URL, most often http: or https:.
search	Represents any query keys and values.
authority	If specified, represents the username, password, and host components of the URL.
directory	Similar to pathname, but includes only the path or directory, not the actual current filename.
domain	Includes the full domain name, port (if specified), and protocol.
filename	Represents the filename, minus the path or directory.
hrefNoHash	If a hash exists, returns the entire original href value, minus the hash character and associated hash value.
hrefNoSearch	If a query string exists, returns the entire original href value, minus the query string.
password	Represents any passwords specified in the URL.
username	Represents any usernames specified in the URL.

To use any of these utilities, simply wait for the page to load and access them through the `$.mobile` object. These utility methods and properties offer quick ways to access or alter data needed when developing with jQuery Mobile. You may even find that you need functionality in addition to these methods and properties and need to create your own set of utilities/custom JavaScript methods to be reused in your application.

WRAPPING **UP**

Accessing exposed methods and properties offers a way to tap directly into the jQuery Mobile framework and interact with code functionality to create customized mobile applications. There's a lot happening behind the scenes with this simple framework, and there are many ways to add custom functionality to provide powerful mobile websites and applications. By tapping into the API you can create any functionality you need.

PART V

JQUERY MOBILE CMS

15

INSTALLING
A MOBILE
WORDPRESS THEME

WordPress is a powerful content management system (CMS) that began as a way to create simple blogs and websites. It's currently used by over 60 million people and growing. WordPress development is in demand and having the ability to create mobile WordPress websites just adds to the appeal. This chapter starts from the beginning, showing you where and how to install WordPress on a web server, then explains where to get the jQuery Mobile WordPress theme and how to install it, and finally shows you how to create new pages and blog posts.

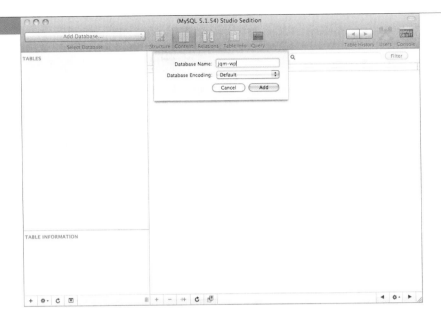

FIGURE 15.1 Adding a database named jqm-wp to store WordPress data.

You have two options when creating a WordPress website. The first is to visit wordpress.com and create a blog on their huge network. The second, and the one we'll be using in this chapter, is to visit wordpress.org and download WordPress to install on your own server using what they call their "famous 5-minute installation." As you'll see in this chapter, it's actually true, but first you need to have a web server and a database installed. If you don't have a web server of your own, WordPress recommends the web hosts listed on http://wordpress.org/hosting/, or you can find a web host of your choice. The only caveat is that your web server needs to have PHP and MySQL to run WordPress.

INSTALLING WORDPRESS

Once you have a web server set up, you'll need to upload the WordPress files and then download a MySQL database to configure WordPress. You can find the WordPress configuration in the wp-config.php file. For the database, there are a number of free MySQL apps you can download and use. For the example in this chapter, we'll use Sequel Pro for Mac OS, which you can download at www.sequelpro.com, and we'll create a database named jqm-wp using Sequel Pro (**Figure 15.1**).

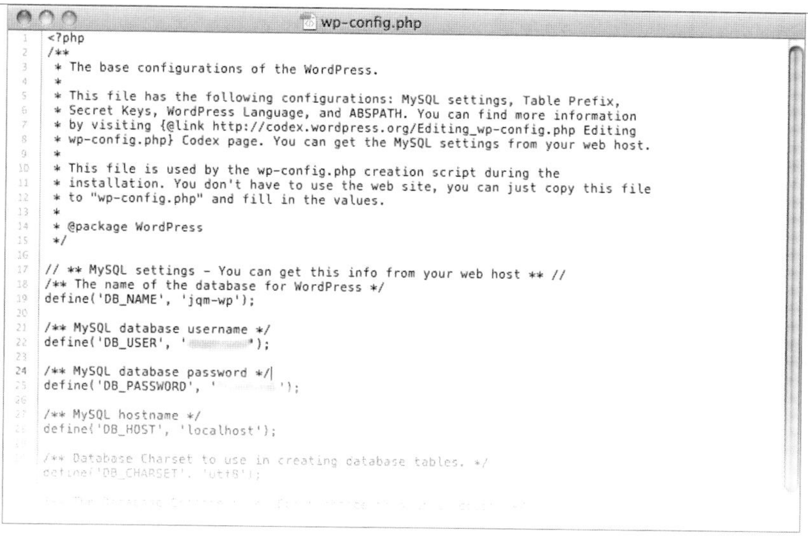

```
<?php
/**
 * The base configurations of the WordPress.
 *
 * This file has the following configurations: MySQL settings, Table Prefix,
 * Secret Keys, WordPress Language, and ABSPATH. You can find more information
 * by visiting {@link http://codex.wordpress.org/Editing_wp-config.php Editing
 * wp-config.php} Codex page. You can get the MySQL settings from your web host.
 *
 * This file is used by the wp-config.php creation script during the
 * installation. You don't have to use the web site, you can just copy this file
 * to "wp-config.php" and fill in the values.
 *
 * @package WordPress
 */

// ** MySQL settings - You can get this info from your web host ** //
/** The name of the database for WordPress */
define('DB_NAME', 'jqm-wp');

/** MySQL database username */
define('DB_USER', '');

/** MySQL database password */
define('DB_PASSWORD', '');

/** MySQL hostname */
define('DB_HOST', 'localhost');

/** Database Charset to use in creating database tables. */
define('DB_CHARSET', 'utf8');
```

FIGURE 15.2 Adding the database connection information to the wp-config.php file.

With the database in place, the last step is to add the database login data to the WordPress configuration file or, as mentioned previously, wp-config.php (**Figure 15.2**). Again, this file is what contains the server configuration data for WordPress. You'll need to at least complete the `DB_NAME`, `DB_USER`, `DB_PASSWORD`, and `DB_HOST` variables to get WordPress to point to your database.

The names are pretty self-explanatory, but it's important to know what they are. **Table 15.1** lists the variable names along with brief descriptions of each.

TABLE 15.1 WordPress database configuration variables

VARIABLE NAME	DESCRIPTION
DB_NAME	The name of the database. As an example, we named our database jqm-wp, as shown in Figure 15.1.
DB_USER	The username you used when setting up the database.
DB_PASSWORD	The password you used when setting up the database.
DB_HOST	The host name for your database. This value is typically `localhost`, but it can sometimes be the same as your domain name or something completely custom based on your web host.

FIGURE 15.3 The WordPress installation process.

With the database set up, visit the site and complete the installation process by adding a site title and creating an admin user (**Figure 15.3**). Remember the password you use when creating this account, because you'll need it when you're finished with the installation.

That's it! With WordPress installed, you can now log in to the WordPress administration area using the username and password you just entered. Within the administration area, you can completely manage your website. For example, you can create webpages, blog posts, and users, as well as install plug-ins and themes. With that said, now it's time to set up the jQuery Mobile theme for our sample website.

CREATING THE JQUERY MOBILE THEME

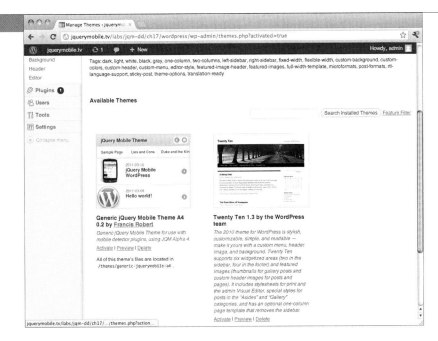

FIGURE 15.4 Activating the jQuery Mobile WordPress theme.

Adding a theme to WordPress is super easy. All you need to do is download, buy, or create a theme, and then upload it to the wp-content/themes directory within your WordPress site. Once there, you need to activate the theme and voilà, you're finished. The following example uses a jQuery Mobile theme from Francis Robert, a freelance web programmer who has the most functional jQuery Mobile WordPress theme I've found to date. You can find it in the WordPress category of his blog at http://frobert.com. (Thanks, Francis! It's great to see developers sharing great things with each other.)

Once you've downloaded the jQuery Mobile theme, you can upload it to the wp-content/themes directory, as mentioned previously. After uploading the theme, log in to the WordPress administration area and visit the Appearance > Themes page from the left sidebar. Once there, select the Activate link under the jQuery Mobile theme (**Figure 15.4**).

FIGURE 15.5 (Left) Configuring the jQuery Mobile WordPress theme.

FIGURE 15.6 (Right) A default WordPress installation with Francis Robert's jQuery Mobile WordPress theme.

Once activated, the WordPress website includes the jQuery Mobile theme, which defaults to the prebuilt "a" theme. To change this, you can visit the Appearance > Editor page from the left sidebar in the WordPress administration area. In the right sidebar of the Editor page, there's a file named preferences.php. Click this file name and it will load into the text area in the center of the page. You can edit this file and save your changes. **Figure 15.5** shows what Edit mode looks like for the jQuery Mobile theme in the WordPress administration area. Editing the $jqtheme value assigns the appropriate jQuery Mobile theme and changes the look of the website.

Once installed, activated, and configured, the jQuery Mobile theme automatically converts the front-end of your WordPress website into a jQuery Mobile WordPress website. **Figure 15.6** shows an example of the default WordPress installation with Francis Robert's jQuery Mobile theme. This is very powerful stuff.

Figure 15.6 also illustrates the sequence that occurs when a visitor selects a linked list item from the home page. The home page includes a default blog post that's titled "Hello world!" By selecting this post as a linked list item, the page transitions to the blog post, where the full description and comments can be read; it's even possible to post comments from this page.

ADDING **BLOG POSTS** AND **PAGES**

To create more pages and blog posts, you simply need to log in to the WordPress administration area. Once logged in, you can manage all of your content from the navigation in the left sidebar. To create a new blog post, select Posts > Add New (**Figure 15.7**).

From this webpage you can add a title and a description, and choose a category and tags. You can save the blog post as a draft or publish it by clicking the blue Publish button in the top-right module. Once published, you can view the blog post by visiting the home page of your WordPress website (**Figure 15.8**).

FIGURE 15.7 (Left) Creating a new blog post.

FIGURE 15.8 (Right) Viewing a new blog post.

FIGURE 15.9 (Left) Creating a new webpage.

FIGURE 15.10 (Right) Viewing a new webpage in the main menu.

To create a webpage in WordPress visit Pages > Add New in the left sidebar (**Figure 15.9**). Just like a blog post you can add a title and description, but with pages you can also select the parent page and set the order of the page as it will appear in the main menu of the website. Once you've finished, publish the webpage by clicking the blue Publish button in the top right module.

When the new page is published, it appears in the main menu at the top of the website (**Figure 15.10**).

By default, the blog posts are listed on the front page by date in descending order. To change what's displayed on the front page, visit Settings > Reading, and set the front page to an actual webpage and the blog posts to a specific webpage

that will act as the blog portion of the website. In this case, the page titled Blog is used (**Figure 15.11**).

Once complete, the page titled Home will be the front page and the page titled Blog will be the page where the blog posts are listed (**Figure 15.12**).

FIGURE 15.11 (Left) Setting the home and blog pages.

FIGURE 15.12 (Right) The final WordPress jQuery Mobile website.

WRAPPING UP

Who would have thought that setting up a mobile content management system would be so easy? Using WordPress and the jQuery Mobile theme discussed in this chapter, you can have a mobile CMS up and running in no time. The fun part is customizing it using the techniques learned throughout this book. WordPress lets you alter theme files to create further customizations. You can literally start editing the theme files and making updates that will affect how your site renders. You can also add custom HTML to your WordPress pages, which can include the widgets covered in this book, such as linked lists, collapsible content, and so on.

16

INSTALLING A MOBILE DRUPAL THEME

Drupal is another content management system (CMS) that powers millions of websites and applications. As with WordPress, you can build blogs, websites, and even enterprise applications by adding your own customizations or by incorporating modules and themes from the Drupal community. This chapter shows you where and how to install Drupal on a web server, then explains where to get the jQuery Mobile Drupal theme and module, how to install them, and how to create new pages.

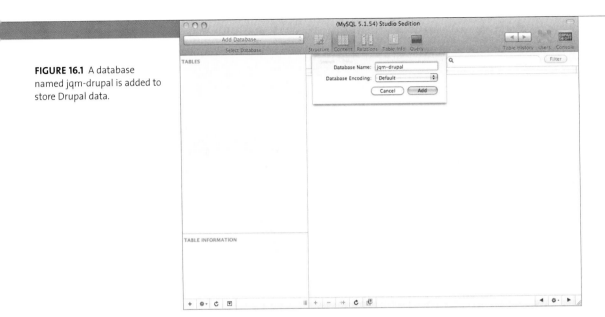

FIGURE 16.1 A database named jqm-drupal is added to store Drupal data.

To get started with Drupal you must first visit the website at www.drupal.org and download the core. The core includes the files needed to run Drupal on a web server. If you don't have a web server of your own, any of the options mentioned in Chapter 15, "Installing a Mobile WordPress Theme," will work. This includes the web hosts listed on http://wordpress.org/hosting/ or any web host of your choice. Again, as with WordPress, the only caveat is that your web server needs to have PHP and MySQL in order to run Drupal.

INSTALLING DRUPAL

Once you have a web server set up, you need to upload the Drupal files then download a MySQL database to configure Drupal. There are a number of free MySQL apps you can download and use for the database. This example uses Sequel Pro for Mac OS, which you'll find at www.sequelpro.com. For the sample in this chapter, we'll be creating a database named jqm-drupal using Sequel Pro, as shown in **Figure 16.1**.

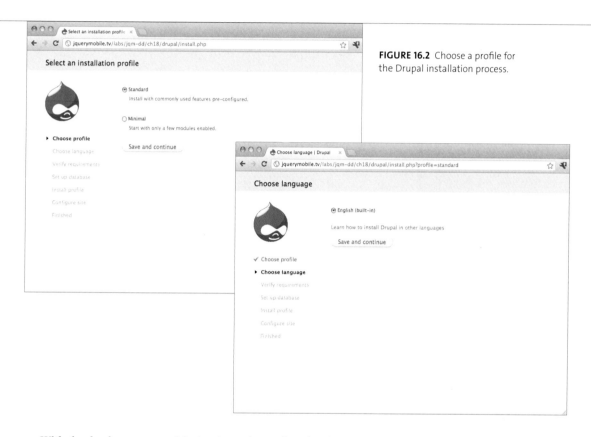

FIGURE 16.2 Choose a profile for the Drupal installation process.

With the database set up, visit the site and complete the six-step installation process. The first step is choosing a profile (**Figure 16.2**). Unless you know exactly what you want, choose the Standard option, because it includes common features to prevent you from wasting your time reinventing the wheel with your Drupal configurations.

Now it's time to choose the language (**Figure 16.3**). By default, English is the only option, but you can click the link in this webpage to learn how to install Drupal in other languages.

FIGURE 16.3 Choose a language for the Drupal installation process.

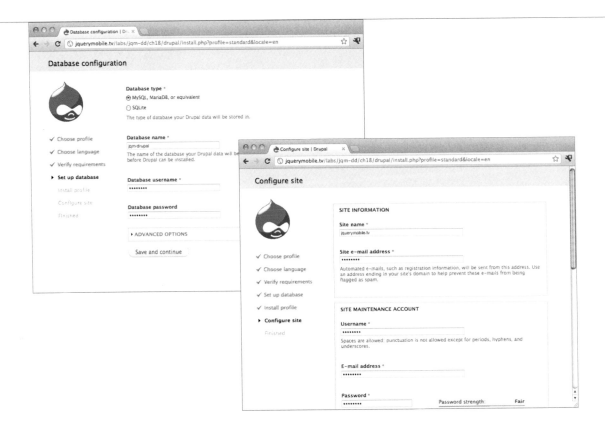

FIGURE 16.4 (Left) The database configuration step of the Drupal installation process.

FIGURE 16.5 (Right) The site configuration step of the Drupal installation process.

After choosing the language, the technical requirements are verified. If the technical requirements do not pass the verification, a list of issues will be displayed. You'll need to address them all before moving to the next installation step. Issues typically consist of simple file permissions that need to be adjusted. Once the verification process is complete, the next step is database configuration (**Figure 16.4**). This step consists of selecting the database type, in this case MySQL. Enter the database login information, including the database name jqm-drupal and the database username and password you used to create the database.

Now it's time to enter your site information (**Figure 16.5**), such as the site name and site e-mail address that will be used for automated e-mails (like registration information), a username, e-mail address, and password for an administrator

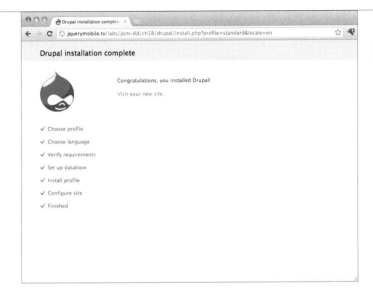

FIGURE 16.6 The Drupal installation process has successfully completed.

account. It's important to remember this login information: You'll need it to log in to the Drupal administration area.

Finally, you'll see a congratulations screen, and you can view your new Drupal website (**Figure 16.6**).

With Drupal installed, you can log in to the Drupal administration area using the username and password you just entered. Within the administration area, you can completely manage your website: You can create webpages, blog posts, and users, as well as install modules and themes. Now it's time to set up the jQuery Mobile theme for our sample website.

THEMING DRUPAL WITH JQUERY MOBILE

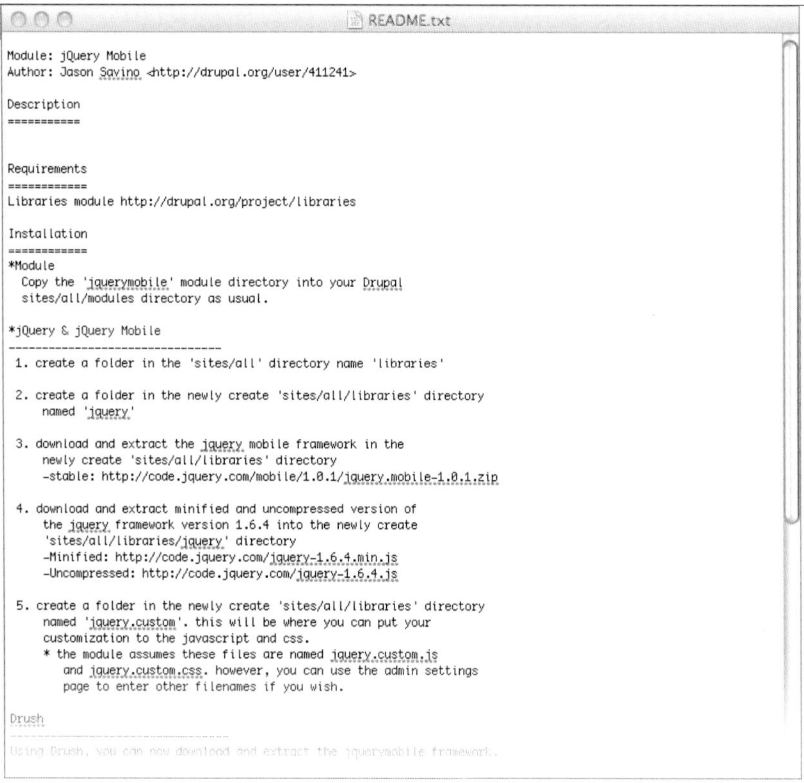

```
Module: jQuery Mobile
Author: Jason Savino <http://drupal.org/user/411241>

Description
===========


Requirements
============
Libraries module http://drupal.org/project/libraries

Installation
============
*Module
  Copy the 'jquerymobile' module directory into your Drupal
  sites/all/modules directory as usual.

*jQuery & jQuery Mobile
--------------------------------
 1. create a folder in the 'sites/all' directory name 'libraries'

 2. create a folder in the newly create 'sites/all/libraries' directory
     named 'jquery'

 3. download and extract the jquery mobile framework in the
     newly create 'sites/all/libraries' directory
     -stable: http://code.jquery.com/mobile/1.0.1/jquery.mobile-1.0.1.zip

 4. download and extract minified and uncompressed version of
     the jquery framework version 1.6.4 into the newly create
     'sites/all/libraries/jquery' directory
     -Minified: http://code.jquery.com/jquery-1.6.4.min.js
     -Uncompressed: http://code.jquery.com/jquery-1.6.4.js

 5. create a folder in the newly create 'sites/all/libraries' directory
     named 'jquery.custom'. this will be where you can put your
     customization to the javascript and css.
     * the module assumes these files are named jquery.custom.js
        and jquery.custom.css. however, you can use the admin settings
        page to enter other filenames if you wish.

Drush
------------------------------------
Using Drush, you can now download and extract the jquerymobile framework.
```

FIGURE 16.7 jQuery Mobile module installation process.

Adding a jQuery Mobile theme to Drupal is fairly easy, but not as easy as with WordPress. Drupal requires two items to be installed to use a jQuery Mobile theme: the jQuery Mobile module and the jQM theme.

INSTALLING THE JQUERY MOBILE MODULE

The jQuery Mobile module was created to enhance the theme and provide admin functionality, such as choosing the framework version, setting swatches, and even theming individual menus and other layout elements. You can find more information about the module at http://drupal.org/project/jquerymobile. Once downloaded, this module needs to be placed into the sites/all/modules/ directory of your Drupal installation. Within the module folder, there's a file named README.txt that lists the steps for completing the installation (**Figure 16.7**).

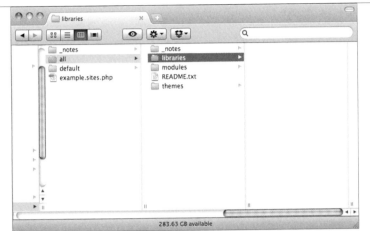

FIGURE 16.8 Create a *libraries* directory.

FIGURE 16.9 Create a *jquery* directory.

The first step in this process is to create a directory named libraries in the sites/all directory (**Figure 16.8**).

Within that directory, create a directory named jquery (**Figure 16.9**).

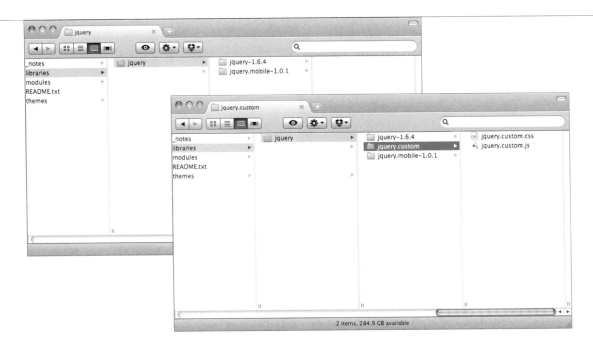

FIGURE 16.10 (Left) Add the jQuery Mobile framework and the jQuery library to the jquery directory.

FIGURE 16.11 (Right) Create a directory named jquery.custom in the jquery directory.

Download and copy the jQuery Mobile framework and jQuery library into the jquery directory you just created (**Figure 16.10**).

Create a directory for custom JavaScript and CSS named jquery.custom and add it to the jquery directory (**Figure 16.11**).

Before activating the module, you have the option to configure any of the jQuery Mobile defaults. You can add and modify the following variables in the settings.php file (the file is located in the settings.php file in the sites/default directory of your Drupal installation):

```
$conf['jquerymobile_front] = 0;

$conf['jquerymobile_ns] = '';

$conf['jquerymobile_autoInitializePage] = '';

$conf['jquerymobile_subPageUrlKey] = '';

$conf['jquerymobile_activePageClass] = '';
```

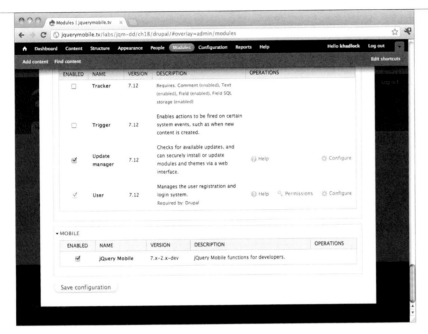

FIGURE 16.12 Activate the jQuery Mobile module.

```
$conf['jquerymobile_activeBtnClass] = '';
$conf['jquerymobile_ajaxEnabled] = '';
$conf['jquerymobile_hashListeningEnabled] = '';
$conf['jquerymobile_defaultPageTransition] = '';
$conf['jquerymobile_defaultDialogTransition] = '';
$conf['jquerymobile_minScrollBack] = '';
$conf['jquerymobile_loadingMessage] = '';
$conf['jquerymobile_pageLoadErrorMessage'] = '';
```

At last it's time to activate the module in the Drupal administration area. Visit the modules section and locate the jQuery Mobile module, which should appear under the Mobile section (**Figure 16.12**).

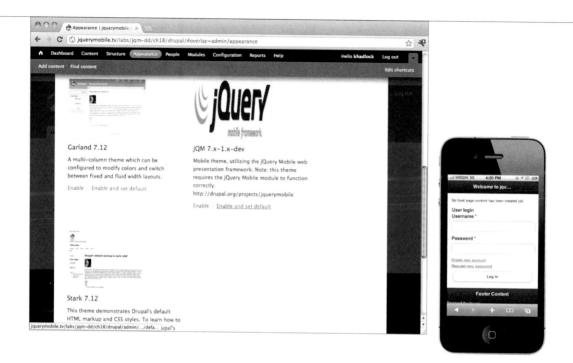

FIGURE 16.13 (Left) Activate the jQuery Mobile theme.

FIGURE 16.14 (Right) A default Drupal installation with the jQuery Mobile theme.

INSTALLING THE JQUERY MOBILE THEME

With the jQuery Mobile module installed, configured, and activated, it's time for the theme. You can download the jQM theme from http://drupal.org/project/jqm. This theme converts the front-end of the website into a jQuery Mobile experience. The theme requires the jquerymobile module, therefore it's important to download and install it before attempting to use this theme. Luckily, we just did this, so now it's time to set up the theme.

With the theme downloaded, place it in the sites/all/themes/jqm/ directory of your Drupal installation. To activate the theme, go to the Appearance page of the Drupal administration area and select the Enable link below the theme (**Figure 16.13**).

By default, the theme will not include any pages or articles, so when you visit the site you will see a login screen. However, you should see that the jQuery Mobile theme is now active and driving the style of your header, footer, text inputs, and buttons (**Figure 16.14**).

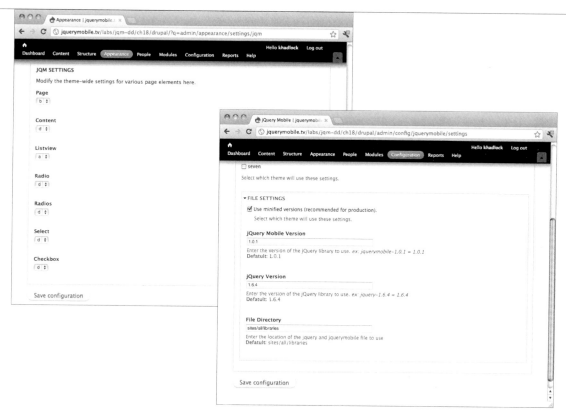

CUSTOM SETTINGS

With the jQuery Mobile module and theme in place, you can customize various settings. The theme lets you configure quite a few swatches for different form elements. If you visit the Appearance page of the Drupal administration area and select the Settings link next to the jQuery Mobile theme, you'll see a list of options under the JQM Settings section shown **Figure 16.15**.

You can also configure settings in the jQuery Mobile module. To edit these settings, visit the Modules page, scroll until you find the jQuery Mobile module, and select the Configuration link next to the module. On this page you'll see an area titled File Settings, shown in **Figure 16.16**. If you select this title, it will expand and reveal text inputs you can use to set the version of the jQuery library and jQuery Mobile framework as well as the file path location for the files that were uploaded to the Drupal installation in Figure 16.10.

FIGURE 16.15 (Left) jQuery Mobile theme settings in a Drupal installation.

FIGURE 16.16 (Right) jQuery Mobile module settings in a Drupal installation.

ADDING **CONTENT**

FIGURE 16.17 (Left) Create
a blog post in Drupal.

FIGURE 16.18 (Right) Drupal
site with a blog post.

To create more pages and blog posts, you need to log in to the Drupal administration area. Here you can manage all your content from the Content page: Select Add
content to choose a content type. On this page, there are two default content types:
Article and Basic page. To create a blog post, select Article, enter a title, and write
your post in the Body field in the web form seen in **Figure 16.17**.

By default, this blog post appears on the home page of your Drupal website
(**Figure 16.18**).

To create a page, go back to Content, select Add Content, and select Basic page.
Use the web form on this page to create your page. In this example, we're creating
a page named Home, which will ultimately become the front page for the website
(**Figure 16.19**).

You can use this new page as the front page for the Drupal installation. To define
a page as the front page, visit the Configuration page, select Site information, and
scroll down until you see Default front page. Here you'll see the URL of your Drupal
website with a text input to enter the node ID of the page you want to use. You can

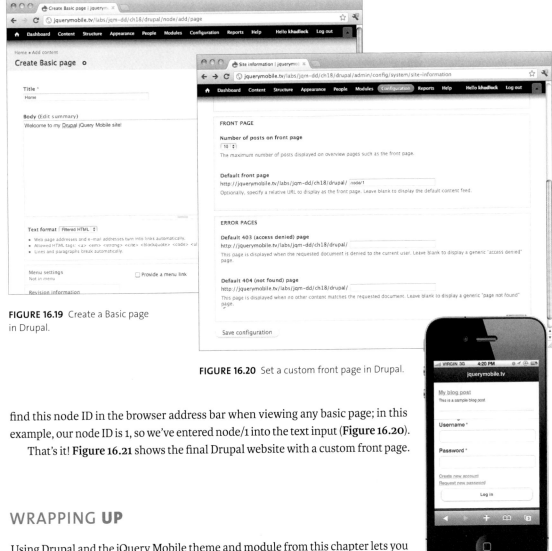

FIGURE 16.19 Create a Basic page in Drupal.

FIGURE 16.20 Set a custom front page in Drupal.

find this node ID in the browser address bar when viewing any basic page; in this example, our node ID is 1, so we've entered node/1 into the text input (**Figure 16.20**).

That's it! **Figure 16.21** shows the final Drupal website with a custom front page.

WRAPPING **UP**

Using Drupal and the jQuery Mobile theme and module from this chapter lets you create a powerful mobile CMS and have it up and running in no time. With the techniques you've learned in this book, you can create unique and custom webpages with widgets, formatting, and other functionality provided by the jQuery Mobile framework. Now there's nothing holding you back from creating a powerful CMS with complete mobile capabilities.

FIGURE 16.21 The final jQuery Mobile Drupal website with a custom front page.

PART VI

BEYOND
jQUERY MOBILE

17

DETECTING
MOBILE **DEVICES**

Mobile websites are often developed separately from primary websites (those intended to be viewed on a desktop or laptop), although they may use much of the same content. To make sure your website is tailored for mobile devices, you'll want to detect when a mobile device visits the site and then redirect the device to markup made especially for mobile. You may also want to deliver a website layout and content based on a specific mobile device. In this chapter, you'll learn how to do both. Let's begin by learning how to detect when a mobile device accesses your website.

USING **PHP**

Since PHP is one of the most popular scripting languages on the web, let's look at a PHP function that performs mobile detection across a wide array of mobile devices. The function is simple and can be extended and modified easily:

```
function mobile_detect(){

    $mobile_devices = '/(alcatel|amoi|android|avantgo|blackberry
|benq|cell|cricket|docomo|elaine|htc|iemobile|iphone|ipad|ipaq|ipod
|j2me|java|midp|mini|mmp|mobi|motorola|nec-|nokia|palm|panasonic
|philips|phone|sagem|sharp|sie-|smartphone|sony|symbian|t-mobile
|telus|vodafone|wap|webos|wireless|xda|xoom|zte)/i';
    if(preg_match($mobile_devices, $_SERVER['HTTP_USER_AGENT'])) {

        return true;

    } else {

        return false;

    }

}
```

The first variable in the function, $mobile_devices, holds a regular expression string that identifies many of the mobile devices in use today. The regular expression is an OR statement with the pipe symbol (|) representing the OR statement

HOW MANY TYPES OF MOBILE DEVICES ARE THERE?

The regular expression string in the example doesn't begin to cover all the mobile devices with unique user agent strings available today. There are literally hundreds of different types of mobile devices capable of surfing websites.

How do you decide which ones to include in your test? Honestly, only you can answer that because it depends on the audience for your mobile website or application.

You'll find many online sources for user agent information. One such source is www.useragentstring.com on which the list of mobile devices is regularly updated and very accurate. You can find the mobile device list at www.useragentstring.com/pages/Mobile Browserlist/.

and separating each device type string. If you were reading it aloud, you might say, "Android or AvantGo or BlackBerry...." The /i at the end of the expression indicates that the search through the string is case-insensitive.

IDENTIFYING THE BROWSER

If you need to add a phone's user agent string, the string that indicates which browser is being used is quite simple. Insert a pipe within the string followed by the phone's user agent string. The list need not be in alphabetical order.

Once you've created your search string, you can test it with PHP's preg_match() function. The first argument in the function is your mobile device string variable holding the regular expression. The second argument is part of PHP's global $_SERVER array, specifically the HTTP_USER_AGENT.

When a web browser makes a request for information from a server, it sends a lot of information about itself to the server to generate the request, including the kind of browser making the request. If the server-side language is PHP (this same information is available in other server-side languages as well), much of the information is stored in the $_SERVER array. This is the key to determining whether a mobile device is accessing your website.

The preg_match() function searches through the regular expression string and looks for a match to the $_SERVER['HTTP_USER_AGENT']. If there's a match, you know a mobile device is accessing your site, and you can handle it appropriately, such as by redirecting the mobile device to the URL where your jQuery Mobile website lives.

LEARNING MORE ABOUT REGULAR EXPRESSIONS

While learning regular expressions may be dreadful and scary, it can be a valuable part of your programming toolkit. Fortunately, there are many resources available online. Here are some recommended websites:

www.regular-expressions.info/ covers a wide range of materials for developing, testing, and using regular expressions.

http://regexlib.com/ provides a searchable library of commonly used regular expressions—perfect for the developer who doesn't want to write his own!

http://regexpal.com/ makes it easy to develop and test regular expressions in real time.

FIGURE 17.1 The web URL in a normal browser and the URL the mobile device is redirected to use.

CALLING THE PHP FUNCTION

To use the PHP mobile detection function you created, you need to call it from the page you expect the mobile device to access. In this example, the function has been saved in a separate file called mobile_detection.php:

```php
include('path/to/mobile_detection.php');

$mobile_device = mobile_detect();

// Perform a redirection if a mobile device is detected

if($mobile_device == true) {

    header('Location: http://m.mywebsite.com');

    exit();

}
```

The code here is fairly self-explanatory. You store the result of the function in a variable named $mobile_device and test that variable to see whether it's true or false. If it's true, you redirect the mobile device's browser to the content you want that device to consume. You can use the function on any page and set custom redirections if you like. The result of the current function redirects the browser to http://m.mywebsite.com, as seen in **Figure 17.1**.

You could return the user agent string from the function so you could perform certain actions based on which kind of device is accessing the website. Rather than do that, let's learn how to detect specific devices with JavaScript when the browser arrives at the mobile site.

USING **JAVASCRIPT** TO
DETECT SPECIFIC **DEVICES**

In some cases, you'll want to know what specific mobile device is accessing your mobile website or application so you can have some control over the user's experience. This control might come in the form of enabling or disabling certain functions or displaying data and content tailored to the user's specific device.

The technique is surprisingly similar to the method we used for PHP. Let's examine a couple of ways to detect a specific mobile device, first using pure JavaScript and then using jQuery.

DETECTING MOBILE DEVICES WITH JAVASCRIPT

In JavaScript, as with PHP, you'll use a regular expression to search through the device's user agent string. From there you can add code to provide specific functionality in your mobile website based on the device accessing the site.

Here's a simple example:

```
var mobile_device = navigator.userAgent.match(/(iPad)|(iPhone)/i);

if(mobile_device) {

    // your code handling specific functionality for these devices

} else {

    // your code to handle functionality outside of these devices

}
```

As you can see, you're using a regular expression to look for a match to the user agent string. JavaScript gathers user agent information in its navigator object, and you can access that information in navigator.userAgent.

On an iPhone 4 using Safari as the browser, the user agent string might look something like this:

```
Mozilla/5.0 (iPhone; U; CPU iPhone OS 4_3_3 like Mac OS X; en-us)
  AppleWebKit/533.17.9 (KHTML, like Gecko) Version/5.0.2 Mobile/8J2
  Safari/6533.18.5
```

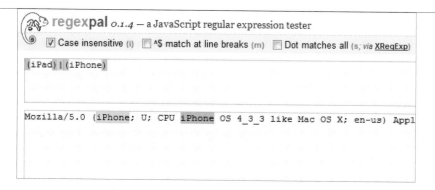

Using JavaScript's `match()` method, you can determine whether the
`navigator.userAgent` has a match in the regular expression `/(iPad)|(iPhone)/i`.
If you were using the tool at http://regexpal.com to test your regular expression, it
would look like **Figure 17.2**.

Now that you know how to test for specific mobile devices, you can build functionality into your site that lets you provide custom information and interactivity
for those devices. Here's a sample of a JavaScript `switch` statement that illustrates
how to code this:

```
var mobile_device = navigator.userAgent;
switch(true) {
    case /(iPad)|(iPod)|(iPhone)/i.test(mobile_device):
        // code for these devices
    break;
    case /(android)/i.test(mobile_device):
        // code for this device
    break;
    default:
        // code for all other devices
    break;
}
```

You can create a case for as many mobile device types and user agent strings as needed to customize and enhance the user experience for anyone who accesses your website with a mobile device.

Keep in mind that regular expression testing and matching can be expensive in terms of processing overhead, so don't get carried away with lots of testing. Be careful when planning and designing your mobile applications so that functionality applies to as broad a range of devices as possible to reduce the number of tests that you make.

NOTE: Visit http://detectmobilebrowsers.com/ for open-source ready-made code in a number of languages that you can build your mobile device detection around.

DETECTING MOBILE BROWSER FEATURES WITH JQUERY

Using pure JavaScript to detect mobile devices is the way to go when you need to know if a mobile device is accessing your website. You can go one step further and determine if a certain browser feature or function is supported with jQuery using jQuery's .support method.

Technically, you can't do device detection with jQuery, but you can determine whether the browser—mobile or otherwise—will support certain features or functionality. This allows you to be browser agnostic during development, instead giving you the ability to account for certain browser features and handle exceptions as needed.

For instance, you may want to know if the browser accessing your site adheres to the World Wide Web Consortium's box model recommendation because portions of your layout rely on that feature. The following jQuery code will determine if the box model feature is true:

```
$.support.boxModel;
```

Now you can handle exceptions with a test:

```
var box_model = $.support.boxModel;
if(!box_model) {
    // place your exception handling code here
}
```

Here's a partial list of the features you can detect using `.support`:

- `ajax` will be `true` if the browser can support XMLHttpRequest.

- `cors` will be `true` if the browser can support a cross-domain XMLHttpRequest.

- `opacity` will be `true` if the browser supports this CSS property (all IE browsers will return false as they use alpha filters).

- `submitBubbles` will be true if a submit event can bubble up the DOM tree.

To find the rest of the list of jQuery `.support` properties, visit http://api.jquery.com/jQuery.support/.

WRAPPING **UP**

Detecting when a mobile device accesses your website and getting specific information about that device could not be easier to do now that you have a solid code foundation for building your jQuery Mobile websites and applications.

You have several good tools available to you for configuring and testing regular expressions and digging deeper into user agent strings. With a firm grasp of these tools, it's easy to develop mobile device detection for any website.

The next question is, "How do I test my websites on as many mobile devices as possible?" Most of us can't afford to purchase all the mobile devices available, so we'll turn our attention to mobile device simulators. That's up next!

18

TESTING WITH SIMULATORS

When it comes to testing mobile websites and applications, you have several options: You can use the browser on the desktop where you develop your markup and code, a mobile device, or a mobile simulator. Each has advantages and disadvantages.

The single largest advantage to testing with a simulator is that you can get immediate feedback on the way your mobile site will look on a mobile device. This will help you tweak your layout and give you clues about how your page-to-page navigation will work.

There's a huge downside. The simulator interaction with your mobile website is drastically different from the interaction on a physical device. You'll miss the touch-enabled features of the device. Your last line of testing should always be done on the kinds of devices you expect that your visitors will actually use.

EXPLORING YOUR TESTING OPTIONS

If you test on the desktop, you can get immediate results. The downside is that, even resized, a desktop web browser won't offer the same experience as a mobile device. For example, scroll bars are much wider and more intrusive on a desktop web browser. Using a desktop browser is good for immediate spot checks.

Most mobile developers have two or three physical devices available for testing, but can't afford to purchase more than that. One solution is "crowd testing," where you ask your friends to access your website or application via their devices and give you feedback about any issues they find. Another solution is using remote labs. Testing in remote labs can be expensive, but it lets you test your sites in multiple devices from the comfort of your desk.

Another option is using a mobile simulator. Mobile simulators are evolving and come in a couple of flavors: ones you work with online and ones you download and install on your desktop. Some simulators come with mobile development tool packages and software development kits (SDK). All typically offer the same sort of immediate feedback that testing on your desktop browser does. The downside is that you can't interact with simulators using gestures available to you on many touch-enabled mobile devices, and sometimes a simulator may not be configured in a way that duplicates the mobile device's browser and operating system.

Let's dig in and find some mobile simulators.

DEVELOPING FOR THE MOBILE WEB

One of the most important questions you need to ask yourself is, who am I developing my mobile website for?

Since you're focused on developing websites and applications using jQuery Mobile, this chapter talks about simulators that deliver the proper experience in a full-fledged mobile web browser typically available on smartphones and pads used by a great many mobile customers today.

There are other simulators available for mobile devices that don't deliver the same kind of experience you'd expect from a fully capable web browser. If you expect that your website visitor will be using these kinds of devices, I strongly recommend that you look into these simulators and learn how to use them as well. Developing for these devices may mean that you have to add code to redirect or strip down your site to accommodate these users.

You should answer the question of who you're designing your mobile website for at the outset of your planning process. Knowing your target audience and the devices you anticipate they use will make development and testing go much more smoothly.

FINDING ONLINE SIMULATORS

FIGURE 18.1 The menu and choices available for the simulator at mobilephoneemulator.com.

Finding solid online mobile device simulators is akin to finding your prince (or princess). You have to kiss a lot of frogs first. Enter "mobile device simulator" into Google, and the results can be staggering and frustrating.

You'll need to take into account that most online simulators are affected by the browser you use to access the simulator. Most online simulators tend to inherit the characteristics of the parent browser and many do not present or honor attributes such as mobile user agent strings or visual elements present in mobile device browsers. We'll talk more about those issues in the "Using Simulators for Testing" section later in this chapter.

Here are some of the better simulators you'll find online:

- **Cowemo at www.mobilephoneemulator.com/**

    The great thing about this mobile emulator is that it offers several different smartphone layouts. The menu allows you to easily switch between mobile devices and orientation, as shown in **Figure 18.1**.

    The screen of the emulator is uncluttered (**Figure 18.2**), making it easy to work with your mobile site. The downside is that the browser inherits the user agent string from the parent browser, making it difficult to test actions that rely on specific mobile devices. Additionally, you can't access sites that

FIGURE 18.2 The uncluttered layout of the website at mobilephoneemulator.com. The user agent string inherited its attributes from the parent browser.

FIGURE 18.3 The Opera Mini simulator.

you may be working with locally (localhost); you must upload your sites to a server accessible from the web.

If you're testing layout, this is a great tool. You can switch between devices quickly. Devices are rendered with the proper screen width and height (there's a mode to enlarge the screen size so you can attend to details), which makes it perfect for capturing screenshots of your sites on different devices.

- **Opera Mini at www.opera.com/developer/tools/mini/**

  Although Opera Mini may not be one of the most widely used browsers, a growing number of people choose to download it and use it instead of the browsers that come packaged with their mobile devices. The online test site (**Figure 18.3**) is clean and easy to use.

  Be aware of the way that Opera Mini interprets Cascading Style Sheets (CSS). Sometimes, more complex layouts aren't rendered as you would expect. It does correctly report most user agent strings if you need those to be

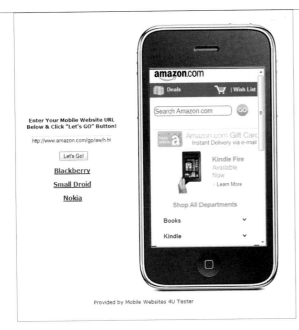

Enter Your Mobile Website URL
Below & Click "Let's GO" Button!

http://www.amazon.com/gp/aw/h.ht

Let's Go!

Blackberry

Small Droid

Nokia

Provided by Mobile Websites 4U Tester

FIGURE 18.4 The desktop's standard scroll bar is used in the Mobile Websites 4U simulator rather than something more befitting a mobile browser.

available when testing, and you must upload your sites to a web-accessible server to test.

- **Mobile Websites 4U at www.mobilewebsites4u.com/tester/**

This simulator is great, but it has some limitations, such as offering only four different screen layouts and inheriting the user agent string from the parent browser. It also uses a desktop browser scroll bar that may affect your site's layout. Have a look at **Figure 18.4**, and you'll see how the scroll bar eats up some screen real estate.

One significant advantage is that you can test from your local machine without having to upload your site files to a web server. Having the ability to quickly check your layout is a real plus for any mobile device emulator.

USING **SIMULATORS** FOR **TESTING**

Now that you have some simulators in your toolbox, it's time to incorporate them into your development workflow. Let's start by testing in the online emulators.

TESTING WITH ONLINE EMULATORS

For most online emulators, all you're required to do is upload your mobile site to a web server, navigate to the online emulator, and type the URL (many will require that you type the `http://` prefix to the URL) into the emulator's address bar. If all is well, you'll see your mobile site in the screen of the simulator.

One thing that will become readily apparent is that you can't interact with desktop simulators in the same way that you would with an actual device. If you're testing with what would normally be a touch-enabled device, you can't perform the same actions like scrolling or zooming with your fingers on the screen of the device. You must use the mouse and keyboard attached to your desktop environment to scroll, click, and otherwise interact with the simulator.

If you designed your mobile site to rely on the user agent string or feature detection, you'll also be missing some key functionality on the desktop device. There are some solutions you can use (see the "Spoofing user agent strings" sidebar) to assist with your testing. You can also determine if the desktop version of the browser matches the mobile browser's feature set. It's important that you load the online simulators into as many different browsers as possible so you can see whether the browser's features will support the programming you've built into your mobile website or application.

Make sure that navigation works as you expect it to. Carefully examine the layout to make sure it fits on the device's screen area. Using online simulators will make it easy to find out whether the site will look good and navigate properly on a mobile device.

There's a solution you can use during the testing process that will let you modify the request header so that the proper user agent strings are sent to the server. You must be using a Mozilla Firefox browser with the Modify Headers add-on. You can get the add-on at:

https://addons.mozilla.org/en-US/firefox/addon/modify-headers/

If you choose to use this tool, you'll want to educate yourself on user agent strings and how to form them. That information is available from the World Wide Web Consortium at:

www.w3.org/Protocols/HTTP/HTRQ_Headers.html

This tool provides a handy user interface that can be easily started from Firefox's add-on toolbar. I encourage you to make it a part of your mobile development toolbox.

USING REMOTE LABS

If you're unable to acquire a group of physical devices to test your mobile websites and applications, you have the option to use a remote lab to test on. The cost of testing and the test experience vary widely from lab to lab, so make sure you do your research before deciding on which lab to use.

Once you've chosen a lab, make sure you have a clearly defined test plan before beginning because many labs charge by the minute or the hour. Make sure you choose your target devices carefully and, once chosen, execute your test plan without getting sidetracked, as every moment counts.

Here are some labs you may want to consider:

- Keynote DeviceAnywhere (www.keynotedeviceanywhere.com) supports over 2,000 devices.

- Paca Mobile Center (www.pacamobilecenter.com) is located in France and is well-stocked with mobile devices.

- Perfecto Mobile (www.perfectomobile.com) currently supports about 500 devices but has aggressive pricing plans.

You generally have two options: Some labs wire the device to a server that's controlled from the tester's computer; others allow you to monitor the test via a remotely accessible camera. This latter approach requires an on-site tester, and the tester will interact with the device. Some labs even offer automated scripted tests.

FIGURE 18.5 Mobilizer offers only four devices, but they are some of the most popular devices available.

TESTING WITH DESKTOP SIMULATORS

Some device manufacturers offer SDKs that let you download and install simulators for testing on your desktop. Some of the most ones popular are Android SDK (developer.android.com/sdk/), BlackBerry (bdsc.webapps.blackberry.com/devzone/), and iPhone simulators that come with XCode (developer.apple.com/xcode/) for use on a Mac.

Another more recently released simulator, available for both Mac and Windows platforms, is called Mobilizer (www.springbox.com/mobilizer/). It is shown in **Figure 18.5**.

Each of these SDKs supports some very specific feature sets and typically does not cover every device available from a particular manufacturer, but using them can give you a quick check of things like layout and navigation.

The test plan for these is similar to that for testing with online emulators. You load your site onto either a local server or a web-accessible server, open the simulator, and type in the URL. Your site should load and you can interact with it using your computer's keyboard and mouse.

The upside is that the SDKs will report user agent strings properly and let you test your site's ability to add or remove features and perform redirections based on what the device's standard browser will support. Testing with a number of them will give you more confidence in the way your site looks and operates before you release it to the public.

CROWD TESTING

My friends like pizza, and they are all passionate about their choices in mobile devices. Put the two together and you have a great resource for a testing party!

Never release your mobile website or application to the public without testing on actual devices. One way to do this is to make friends with people who own and use various phones and pads and get them together for a little crowd testing.

The rules of crowd testing are the same as other forms of testing: You must have a plan. (And never serve the pizza until the test is complete.) You may want to define the plan on a short questionnaire that you give to the crowd or that you can fill out when you're performing one-off hallway testing. Ask the tester to follow the plan, answer the questions about interacting with your site, and make sure the layout meets expectations. You'll also get feedback on the look and feel of your site that can be valuable as you push toward launch.

NOTE: There are crowd-sourced testing services available like Mob4Hire (www.mob4hire.com). They offer a wide range of services and can help guide you through the testing process.

WRAPPING **UP**

There are a lot of options for testing your mobile websites and applications, and you'll have to be diligent in setting up and using simulators with well-defined test plans to ensure success.

As a developer, you'll likely include a combination of online and desktop simulators in your workflow to test the functions and features of the mobile websites you develop. Once you've reached a certain stage of development, you may want to extend your testing to mobile labs (if they are in your budget).

The one simulation you'll always want to include is interacting with your mobile sites on as many physical devices as possible. This can be limited to the devices that are immediately available to you or can involve getting your friends and acquaintances together for a round or two of hands-on examination. Don't forget the pizza!

INDEX

Q

queue methods
  clearQueue, 13–14
  delay, 13
  dequeue, 13
  queue, 13
  using, 14

R

radio buttons, 141–145
  applying mini, 145
  versus checkboxes, 141
  controlgroup data-role groups, 142
  disable method, 145
  enable method, 145
  events, 145
  horizontal toggle set, 143–144
  legend in fieldset, 142
  questions, 142
  refresh method, 145
  setting theme, 145
  statements, 142
  versus text inputs, 145
ready event, using with documents, 11–12
regular expressions
  in JavaScript, 257–259
  learning about, 255
  library of, 255
  testing, 255
  websites, 255
remote labs
  Keynote DeviceAnywhere, 269
  Paca Mobile Center, 269
  Perfecto Mobile, 269
responsive design, considering, 196
Roberts, Francis, 232

S

Save button. *See also* buttons
  adding to header element, 78–80
  combining with Delete, 80

scripts, including, 6
scroll events
  lazy loading effect, 197–199
  scrollstart, 197
  scrollstop, 197
SDKs (software development kits)
  Android, 270
  benefits, 270
  BlackBerry, 270
  XCode, 270
search filter bar, creating, 122–125
search filter text
  changing, 124
  custom formatted listview, 125–128
  mobileinit event, 124–125, 130
  updating, 124
search filters
  custom callback function, 129–130
  customizing, 126–131
  defaultSearch function, 128–129
  filterCallback option, 126
  id for listview, 126–128
  logging text, 129
  pageinit event, 126–128
  testing with searchValue, 129
select menus, 146–151
  action sequence, 146
  controlgroup in, 149
  corners option, 150
  in fieldcontain, 147
  formatting, 147
  grouping, 148–149
  horizontally grouped, 149
  icon option, 150
  iconpos option, 150
  iconshadow option, 150
  initSelector option, 150
  inline option, 150
  methods, 151
  mini option, 150
  nativeMenu option, 150
  open method, 151
  options, 150
  overlayTheme option, 150